CURTIS GRACE
encore
COLLECTION FROM A KENTUCKY COOK

McClanahan
Publishing House

International Standard Book Number 0-913383 58 9
Library of Congress Catalog Card Number 98-84348

Permission for background cover design granted by ©Covington Fabrics.
Cover design and book layout by James Asher Graphics.
Illustrations by Norma Grace.

Manufactured in the United States of America.

All book order correspondence should be addressed to:

McClanahan Publishing House, Inc.
P. O. Box 100
Kuttawa, KY 42055
1-800-544-6959
email: kybooks@apex.net

To Miss Jean, James, and Lil

W
ithout these three devoted, hard-working people, my work load would not have been as easy
and desirable. All worked 30 years plus.
Even though we have retired we still do small parties for
customers we have had for years. James has moved out of
state, yet all we have to do is call and he will be here.
One of our most memorable parties was catering in New
Orleans. What a thrill just being asked. After finishing
the party, we turned it into a mini vacation. Thanks
Mary!

Introduction

A friend once told me how nice it was for me to turn a hobby into a livelihood. I am very thankful I was able to do this. I have always enjoyed cooking and entertaining, even as a young child. My parents both worked and I would usually have "supper" ready when they came home from work.

Once I cut one of my father's prize country hams and took kids on a picnic.

Even though I am retired, I still enjoy doing small things for my beloved customers.

Curtis Grace

Contents

Appetizers

Grace Lake House

Dot's
Crispy Artichoke Hearts

1 cup buttermilk
1/4 cup flour
1/3 teaspoon all-seasoning salt
12 artichoke hearts,
    with "choke" scraped away
Light and fine bread crumbs
Shredded Parmesan cheese
Garlic Hollandaise Sauce

Combine buttermilk, flour and all-seasoning in a bowl and mix well. Dip artichoke heart in batter then roll in bread crumbs, coating heart entirely. Refrigerate for 2 hours. Deep fry at 350° until golden brown. Place several on an appetizer plate and sprinkle with Parmesan cheese. Serve with Garlic Hollandaise Sauce dabbed on top.

Garlic Hollandaise Sauce

3 egg yolks
2 tablespoons lemon juice
Dash cayenne
1/2 teaspoon garlic salt
1/2 cup butter or margarine

Place egg yolks, lemon juice, cayenne and garlic salt in blender container. Cover, quickly turn blender on and off. Heat butter until melted and almost boiling. Turn blender on high speed; slowly pour in butter, blending until thick and fluffy, about 30 seconds.

Makes 1 cup sauce

Artichoke Appetizers

4 eggs, beaten
2 jars marinated artichoke hearts,
  drained and chopped
12 crackers, crumbled
9 ounces cheddar cheese, grated
Salt, pepper and Tabasco to taste

Mix all ingredients together and bake in an eight inch square glass pan which has been sprayed with a nonstick spray. (Metal pans will turn the artichokes dark.) Bake at 325° 30 to 40 minutes or until firm. To serve, cut into squares.

Miss Jean kept saying she was going to take her camera along on one of our parties to capture our food table. When she did take it and started to take a picture she had brought along her remote control for her television instead of her camera. I told her I was sure Miss Kizzie was home trying to change channels with the camera remote.

Artichoke Spread

1 large can artichoke hearts,
  chopped fine
1 small can green chilies, chopped fine
1/2 cup Parmesan cheese
1/2 cup mayonnaise

Mix all together early in the day and refrigerate
to blend flavors. Bake at 350° for 40 minutes in
an 8x8 inch glass pan which has been coated with
cooking spray. Serve with sesame seed crackers.

Carla's Shrimp Dip Mold

3/4 cup boiling water
1 small package lemon gelatin
1 tablespoon lemon juice
3 tablespoons horseradish
1 package unflavored gelatin,
    dissolved in 1/4 cup cold water
12-ounce bottle chili sauce
2 4-ounce cans shrimp, drained

Dissolve lemon gelatin in boiling water, cool slightly; add remaining ingredients and pour into well oiled 3 1/2 cup mold. Chill until set. Serve with club crackers.

People ask if I have ever been late for a party and my reply is "No, but I have been a month early."

Our caravan of people, food, dishes, etc. pulled into the driveway to find the host and hostess working on their lawn. They were as surprised as we were to discover we were a month early. I had to have someone drive me home — I was too weak!

Imy's Eight Layer Dip

1 can jalapeño bean dip
1 can frozen guacamole dip
1/2 cup mayonnaise
   plus 1/2 cup sour cream, mixed
1/2 package taco mix
1 to 3 tomatoes, chopped
Shredded cheddar cheese
Chopped green onions
Sliced black olives

Layer ingredients in a 9" glass pie pan starting with bean dip on bottom and ending with olives on top. Serve with Fritos for dipping.

Spicy Onion Dip

1 yellow onion
2 beef bouillon cubes
1/2 teaspoon cayenne pepper
1 tablespoon Worcestershire sauce
8 ounces sour cream

Dice onions and sauté in a little olive oil until clear. Add bouillon cubes, crush and cook until dissolved. Add Worcestershire and cayenne pepper and cool. Mix with sour cream until smooth. Chill until needed. Serve with chips or vegetable sticks.

Serves 6

Spinach Dip

10-ounce package frozen chopped spinach
1 cup mayonnaise
1 cup sour cream
1 5/8-ounce package vegetable soup mix
6-ounce can water chestnuts,
   chopped or thinly sliced
Small amount of chopped onion

Thaw spinach and drain until barely moist.
Combine mayonnaise, sour cream and soup mix.
Add spinach, water chestnuts and chopped onion.
Mix well and let stand several hours in refrigerator. Serve with crackers.

Crab Meat Dip

8-ounce package cream cheese, softened
1/2 cup mayonnaise
2 tablespoons Worcestershire sauce
2 tablespoons horseradish
2 tablespoons chili sauce
1 can crab meat, rinsed and drained

Mix all ingredients together and serve with crackers for dipping. If too stiff, add a little cream.

Baked Pâté Cedaredge

1 1/2 pounds chicken livers
1/2 pound veal stew meat
1 medium onion, chopped
1 clove garlic, minced
4 tablespoons butter
2 eggs
1/4 cup all-purpose flour
1/2 teaspoon ginger
1/2 teaspoon allspice
Salt and pepper to taste
1 cup heavy cream

Sauté chicken livers, veal, onions and garlic in butter. Place in food processor with remaining ingredients and process until smooth. Pour into buttered and floured 1 1/2 quart baking pan. Cover tightly and bake in 325° oven 1 1/2 to 2 hours. Chill and unmold onto platter. Serve with crackers.

Serves 6 to 8

Crab Pâté

1 can cream of mushroom soup
1 envelope unflavored gelatin
3 tablespoons cold water
3/4 cup mayonnaise
8 ounces cream cheese,
    room temperature
6 1/2-ounce can crab meat
    (or may use shrimp)
2 tablespoons grated onion
1 cup chopped celery
2 tablespoons chopped parsley
1 teaspoon dill weed

Heat soup; dissolve gelatin in cold water and add
to soup. Stir until dissolved. Add remaining ingredients, stirring well to blend. Place into mold that
has been coated with mayonnaise. Refrigerate
until firm. Unmold on bed of greens. Serve with
crackers.

Mushroom Pâté

1 pound chicken livers
1 pound fresh mushrooms,
   washed and sliced
3/4 pound butter, softened
1/2 cup green onions, chopped
1/2 teaspoon thyme
1/2 teaspoon salt
1/8 teaspoon nutmeg
1/2 cup cognac
Parsley sprigs for garnish

In a large skillet, sauté chicken livers and mushrooms in 1/4 pound of the butter until livers are
no longer pink. With slotted spoon, remove livers
and mushrooms to a blender or food processor.
Reduce liquid in skillet, then add to liver–mushroom mixture along with onions and remaining butter. Blend and add seasonings, then the cognac.
Adjust seasonings, adding more cognac if desired.
Blend until smooth and pour into a 3 cup mold
that has been lightly oiled. Cover and chill until
firm. Unmold, garnish with parsley and serve
with plain crackers or melba rounds.

Serves 12 to 14

Calcuttas

12 large prunes
Port wine
Major Grey's Chutney
Sliced bacon

Soak prunes overnight in Port wine. Drain and dry, then remove pits. Fill prunes with chutney. Wrap with bacon and broil until crisp. Stick with pick and serve warm.

Did you know......

Oats are an easy and safe dietary means of lowering blood cholesterol. Combined with a low or modified-fat diet, cholesterol levels can return to normal. Nineteen young adults with normal cholesterol levels experienced an average 5.3 percent drop in cholesterol when they added two oat bran muffins a day to their regular diets. To add oats to your diet try:

Substitute oat bran for up to one-third of the flour in baked goods.
Add 2 tablespoons of regular or quick cooking rolled oats to two cups of brown rice and use as a side dish
Toast rolled oats with a bit of oil and cinnamon in a 350° oven and serve as a topping for low-fat yogurt or cottage cheese.
Substitute oat bran for bread crumbs in meatloaf (1/3 cup for every pound of meat.

Chocolate-Orange Cream Cheese Stuffed Dates

20 dates, pitted
1/4 cup semi-sweet chocolate chips
1/4 cup light cream cheese
1/2 teaspoon grated orange peel
1/2 teaspoon vanilla or Grand Marnier
3 tablespoons finely chopped
   toasted walnuts

Slice each date open lengthwise and set aside.
Melt chocolate chips in top of double boiler over
simmering water, or in microwave oven. Stir until
just melted and remove from heat. Meanwhile,
mix together cream cheese, orange peel and vanilla
or Grand Marnier until well combined. Stir in
melted chocolate, mixing until smooth. Stir in walnuts. Using a small spoon, fill each date with
approximately 3/4 teaspoon mixture. Chill stuffed
dates in refrigerator for one hour. Roll in sugar
before serving.

Pecan & Lemon Cream Cheese Stuffed Dates

24 pitted dates
2 ounces light cream cheese
1 teaspoon sugar, plus extra for rolling
1 teaspoon lemon juice
1/4 teaspoon grated lemon peel
Pinch ground cloves
24 toasted pecan halves

Slice each date open lengthwise, set aside. Mix together remaining ingredients except pecans until well blended. Using a small spoon, fill each date with 1/2 teaspoon cream cheese and one pecan half. Chill for one hour. Roll in sugar.

Susan's Mock Oysters

1/4 pound butter
1/2 large onion, chopped
1 large can mushroom pieces, drained
3 stalks celery, chopped
1 green pepper, chopped
1 package frozen chopped broccoli
1 package Kraft garlic cheese
1 can cream of mushroom soup, undiluted

Melt butter; sauté onion, mushroom pieces, celery
and pepper. Cook broccoli as directed, drain well.
Blend broccoli and onion mixture. Add cheese and
stir until melted. Stir in soup. Serve as a dip or
vegetable or spread on finger sandwiches and heat
in oven.

Party
Pimiento Cheese Spread

2 pounds sharp cheese
3 cloves garlic
7-ounce jar pimientos, undrained
1/2 bottle Durkee's dressing
2 cups mayonnaise
2 tablespoons lemon juice
1/2 teaspoon Worcestershire sauce
1/2 teaspoon cayenne pepper
1 teaspoon dry mustard

Cut cheese into 1 1/2 inch cubes and grate about
1/3 at a time in food processor using metal blade.
Remove each 1/3 of grated cheese before adding the
next. To the last third of grated cheese, add garlic
cloves and pimientos. When well mixed, add dressing, mayonnaise, lemon juice, Worcestershire sauce,
cayenne and mustard. Add remainder of cheese and
mix well. Makes about 2 quarts and keeps in the
refrigerator indefinitely. It is suggested you use
Hellmann's or homemade mayonnaise.

Curried Cheese Spread with Chutney

6 ounces cream cheese
8 ounces sharp cheddar cheese spread
3 tablespoons sherry
1/2 teaspoon curry
1/4 teaspoon salt
10 ounces chutney
1/4 cup minced scallions
Crushed peanuts, if desired

Mix all ingredients except chutney and onions with an electric beater. Spread in a shallow dish and chill until firm. Before serving spread chopped chutney over cheese mixture and cover with green onions and crushed peanuts if desired. Serve with wheat or rye crackers.

Makes 10 servings

Ursula's Boursin Cheese

8 ounces cream cheese, softened
1/4 cup butter
1 clove garlic, minced
1 teaspoon milk
1 teaspoon fresh snipped parsley
1/2 teaspoon Herb de Provence
1/4 teaspoon red wine vinegar
1/4 teaspoon Worcestershire sauce

Combine all ingredients in food processor or mixer.
Beat until smooth. Refrigerate 12 hours.
Remove 1/2 hour before serving.

Herb de Provence

3 tablespoons marjoram
1 1/2 teaspoons rosemary
3 tablespoons thyme
3 tablespoons summer savory
1/2 teaspoon sage

Mix and store in jar with a tightly closed lid.
This herb mixture is also good in salads, dips and
on fowl and fish.

Walnut Chili Cheese Ball

1 pound natural cheddar cheese
1 cup black walnuts
6 ounces cream cheese
1/2 teaspoon garlic powder
1 tablespoon Worcestershire sauce
2 tablespoons minced onion
Chili powder

Grind together cheese and walnuts. Blend in cream cheese and remaining ingredients, except chili powder. Form into ball and roll in chili powder. Sprinkle with additional black walnuts, if desired.

Christeen's Salmon Mousse with Dill Sauce

2 envelopes unflavored gelatin
1/2 cold water
1/2 cup mayonnaise
1/3 cup lemon juice
1/2 cup creamed cottage cheese
Dash Tabasco sauce
16 ounces red salmon,
    skin and bones discarded
2/3 cup heavy cream, whipped
1/2 cup minced celery
3 tablespoons minced onions
4 tablespoons minced parsley
2 boiled eggs, chopped

Soak gelatin in cold water, then dissolve over hot water. Blend mayonnaise, lemon juice, cottage cheese and Tabasco well in mixer. Add gelatin mixture and chill until it begins to set. Add salmon to mixture and stir only to blend. Fold in whipped cream and remaining ingredients. Place in a mold coated with mayonnaise and chill overnight. Serve with Dill Sauce.

Dill Sauce

1 cup sour cream
1/2 cup mayonnaise
1 tablespoon dried dillweed
   or 2 tablespoons fresh

Combine all ingredients.

Did you know.....

2+ quarts of strawberries or 3 honeydew melons have fewer calories than 1 cup of ice cream?

Tub margarine is better for you than stick margarine?

A cup of canned shrimp or 9 whole tomatoes have less fat than 2 tablespoons of regular mayonnaise?

The dark meat of chicken and turkey has more than twice the fat of the light meat?

A 5 pound sack of Idaho potatoes has less fat than 10 roasted peanuts?

A spoonful of corn syrup has nearly 25% more calories than a spoonful of white sugar?

Sis Michael's Del Monte Mousse

2 packages unflavored gelatin
1/2 cup cold water
1 cup rich, hot, chicken broth
2 tablespoons grated onion
2 tablespoons lemon juice
1/2 teaspoon salt
1/8 teaspoon pepper
8 ounces cream cheese,
    crumbled or whipped
13 ounces tuna, packed in water
2 egg whites, beaten stiff
1 cup mayonnaise
1 cup diced cucumbers
1/4 teaspoon paprika

Dissolve gelatin in water. Add to hot broth, mix in seasonings, blend well. Add cheese. Drain and flake tuna, add to gelatin mixture, mixing well. Chill until thickened. Fold in stiffly beaten egg whites. Chill until firm. Place in individual molds or ring mold. Combine mayonnaise, diced cucumber and paprika. Serve with mold.

Serves 8 to 10

From my dear friend and proof reader.

Crab Ring St. Anthony

2 tablespoons gelatin
1 can Campbell's tomato soup
9 ounces cream cheese
1 cucumber
1 cup mayonnaise
1 teaspoon grated onion
1 large stalk celery
4 cups crab meat
1 teaspoon salt
Cayenne

Soak gelatin in cold water. Bring soup to a boil,
dissolve gelatin in soup, then mix with riced cheese.
Put vegetables through food chopper. (Cut fine.)
Combine all together with crab meat, add seasonings, pour into oiled mold. Chill until firm, remove
to salad platter. Garnish with stuffed eggs, marinated asparagus tips, sliced cucumbers, artichoke
hearts placed in lettuce cups. Serve with thousand
island dressing.

Mayonnaise Dressing

1 teaspoon dry mustard
1 teaspoon salt
2 tablespoons lemon juice
1 teaspoon powdered sugar
2 egg yolks
2 tablespoons vinegar
1 1/2 cups olive oil

Thousand Island Dressing

1 cup mayonnaise
1/3 cup chili sauce
2 tablespoons chopped green peppers
1 tablespoon chopped chives
1 tablespoon chopped pimiento
1/2 cup whipped cream

Combine all ingredients.

Cousin Ruth's Crab Meat Puffs

2 egg whites
6 1/2 ounces canned crab meat,
  rinsed and drained
1 cup mayonnaise
1/2 teaspoon seasoned salt
1/4 teaspoon black pepper,
  freshly ground
1/2 teaspoon Worcestershire sauce
2 teaspoons grated onion
Bread rounds, toasted on one side

Beat egg whites; fold in crab meat, mayonnaise and seasonings. Spoon crab meat mixture on toasted side of bread rounds. Broil 3 minutes or until brown and puffy. Serve immediately.

For an interesting and delicious hors d'oeuvre, cut cold cornbread dressing into bite size squares. Watch for looks of satisfaction from your guests! A good holiday treat.

Crab Tarts

1 can crab meat, rinsed and drained
1 tablespoon lemon juice
1 cup chopped celery
1/4 cup chopped green onions
1/2 cup shredded sharp cheese
1/2 teaspoon Tabasco sauce
1/4 teaspoon seasoned salt

Sprinkle lemon juice over crab meat. Add remaining ingredients, blend and spoon into tiny tart pans that have been lined with sharp cheese pastry.

Sharp Cheese Pastry

1 stick butter, softened
1 cup grated sharp cheese
1 cup flour
Dash black pepper and seasoned salt
Few drops Tabasco

Mix cheese and butter. Introduce flour and seasonings to cheese-butter mixture and press into tart pans. Spoon crab mixture into lined tart pans and bake at 350° for 20 to 25 minutes.

Eggplant Caviar

1 medium eggplant
1 onion, finely minced
1 clove garlic, minced
1 tomato, peeled, chopped and drained
1 teaspoon sugar
2 tablespoons vinegar
3 tablespoons olive oil
Salt and pepper to taste

Boil whole eggplant until tender. Cool, eggplant and chop finely. Add remaining ingredients, mix well and chill. Spread on buttered slices of rye bread or crisp toasted rounds.

Garden Gold Cheese Puffs

2 tablespoons butter or margarine
1 small onion, chopped
3 tablespoons flour
1 cup milk
1 teaspoon salt
1/2 teaspoon dry mustard
1/4 teaspoon pepper
8-ounce package cream cheese, crumbled
4 eggs separated
1 cup greens, (turnip or mustard),
    cooked, chopped and drained

Melt butter in saucepan over low heat. Add
onion and cook slowly for 5 minutes. Stir in flour,
then milk. Add salt, dry mustard and pepper.
Cook and stir until very thick; cool slightly. Mix
in cream cheese, egg yolks and greens. Beat egg
whites until stiff but not dry; fold into greens
mixture. Pour into an ungreased 2 quart casserole. Bake at 325° for approximately 2 hours or
until knife inserted into the center comes out
clean.

Serves 6

New Orleans Diablotins

1 cup crumbled Roquefort cheese
1/4 pound butter or margarine, softened
1/2 cup finely ground walnuts—
  (do not substitute)
Generous pinch cayenne pepper
16 slices French bread

Combine cheese, walnuts and pepper. Trim crusts
from slices of French bread, then cut into 3 long
strips about 1 inch wide. Spread butter lightly on
one side and toast; spread the cheese mixture generously on unbuttered side and broil briefly, until
very lightly browned.

Yield: 48 strips

Reuben Tarts

12 ounces cream cheese
3/4 cup margarine
1 1/2 cups plain flour
1/2 cup mayonnaise
1/4 cup chili sauce
16-ounce can sauerkraut, drained
8-ounce can corned beef
3/4 cup grated Swiss cheese
Paprika

Blend cheese, margarine and flour. Chill one hour.
Shape in small balls and place in ungreased muffin
tins. Press dough on bottom and sides of cups.
Mix remaining ingredients for filling. Fill cups
and sprinkle with paprika. Bake at 350° until
brown.

Makes 18 to 24 tarts

Ruth's Clam Rolls

Sandwich bread
Melted butter
2 tablespoons minced onion
2 tablespoons butter
Dash Worcestershire sauce
Salt
Pepper
Dash garlic salt
1 tablespoon flour
7-ounce can minced clams, undrained

Trim crust from sandwich bread. Roll very thin with rolling pin. Spread with melted butter and set aside.

Cook minced onion in butter. Add Worcestershire sauce, salt and pepper to taste, and garlic salt. Stir in flour and add clams. Bring mixture to boil and cook for 1 minute. Spread on slices of bread and roll. Refrigerate until ready to use. Cut in half and brush with melted butter. Bake at 400° about 10 minutes until light brown. Serve hot.

At a cocktail party Dr. Sam French said,
"If any of these are left over, send them to heaven."

Sauerkraut Balls

4 tablespoons butter or margarine
1 medium size onion, finely chopped
1/2 pound cooked ham, diced
1/2 clove garlic, minced
1/3 cup flour
1/2 cup chicken bouillon
3 cups canned, drained,
   chopped sauerkraut
1 tablespoon chopped parsley
1 egg
1/2 cup milk
1/3 cup flour
1 cup fine dry bread crumbs

Sauté onion in melted butter or margarine until light brown. Add ham and garlic; brown lightly. Blend in flour. Stir in bouillon, sauerkraut and parsley; mix and cook, stirring constantly until mixture is thick. Spread in a pan. Chill in refrigerator. When ready to fry; form into balls 1/2 to 1" diameter. Beat egg and milk together. Dip balls in flour, then egg mixture, then bread crumbs. Fry a few at a time in deep hot fat about 2-3 minutes until golden brown. Freezes well before or after frying.

Makes 50 to 60 balls

Snow Pea Pods Stuffed with Sesame Pork

8 ounces cooked pork, diced small
1 scallion, finely chopped
1/4 cup fresh bean sprouts,
 blanched and finely chopped
1 tablespoon diced sweet red pepper
1/2 cup fresh diced water chestnuts
1 tablespoon soy sauce
1 tablespoon oyster sauce
A few dashes of sesame oil
20 fresh pea pods, cleaned,
 with threads removed

Toss together pork, scallion, bean sprouts, red pepper, water chestnuts, soy sauce, oyster sauce and sesame oil. Place pea pods in boiling salted water for approximately 45 seconds, remove immediately and plunge into <u>ice cold</u> water to stop the cooking process. With a sharp paring knife, split open the pods on the straight side, so that they resemble little canoes. Fill pods generously with pork mixture.

Supa Chalupas

6 ounces corn chips
8-ounce can chili with beans
3 ounces shredded
    Monterey Jack cheese
3 ounces shredded cheddar cheese
Handful shredded lettuce
1 ounce sliced Jalapeños
1 ounce sliced black olives
2 ounces diced tomatoes
1 ounce chopped green onions
2 ounces sour cream
2 ounces guacamole

Place chips on large oval platter, cover with chili then cheeses. Top with lettuce, jalapeños, olives, tomatoes, green onions, sour cream and then guacamole. Could also be served individually as a luncheon dish.

Beverages

Grace Episcopal church Steeple
norma grace

Grace Episcopal Church

Coffee Punch

1 gallon strong sweetened coffee,
    chilled (regular or decaffeinated)
1 gallon chocolate, vanilla ice cream
    or chocolate swirl
1 pint whipped cream
Pinch salt
1 cup rum

Scoop ice cream into punch bowl. Add whipped cream, coffee, salt and a punch cup of rum. Fold gently.

One cup instant coffee with 3 cups sugar and water to yield 1 gallon may be used to make strong coffee. Also, 1/2 gallon of each flavor ice cream may be used.

Serves 30 to 40

Vodka Punch

46 ounces unsweetened pineapple juice
46 ounces unsweetened grapefruit juice
6 ounces frozen lemonade concentrate
6 ounces frozen orange juice concentrate
33 ounces club soda
1 fifth vodka

Mix all ingredients except club soda. Pour over ice ring in punch bowl. Add club soda just before serving. Garnish punch with thinly sliced lemons, oranges and maraschino cherries.

Serves 20

Nice to serve in hot summertime.

Milk Punch

For 8 to 10 servings:
1 quart milk
1 quart ginger ale
1 pint sherbet

For 50 servings:
1 gallon milk
1 gallon ginger ale
2 quarts sherbet

Place semi-soft sherbet in punch bowl. Add milk and ginger ale. Stir until sherbet floats in small pieces throughout. Garnish with maraschino cherries or sliced strawberries, fresh sprigs of mint, shredded pineapple, or orange slices, as desired.

Miss Mama's Hot Spiced Percolator Punch

9 cups unsweetened pineapple juice
9 cups cranberry juice
4 1/2 cups water
1 cup brown sugar
4 1/2 teaspoons whole cloves
4 sticks cinnamon
1/4 teaspoon salt

Place juices and water in the bottom of a 30-cup percolator. In top basket, place sugar, spices, and salt. Plug in and perk! Very good!

Serves 36 (1/2 cup servings)

Rum Punch

1 cup sugar
1 cup water
1 cup lime juice
1 1/2 bottles (fifths) rum
2 quarts sparkling water
2 cups pineapple juice

Boil sugar and water for 10 minutes. Let cool and add lime juice, pineapple juice and rum. Mix the day before serving. When ready to serve, pour over ice ring in punch bowl. Garnish with thinly sliced limes and maraschino cherries. Just before serving, add sparkling water.

Serves 32

Jo's Banana Punch

6 bananas, mashed
6-ounce can
   frozen orange juice concentrate
6-ounce can
   frozen lemonade concentrate
4 cups sugar
7 cups water
A few drops of yellow food coloring
Ginger ale, chilled

Mix and freeze all ingredients except ginger ale.
Remove from freezer 2 hours before serving time.
Length of time can depend on temperature. Place
in punch bowl and add ginger ale to fill bowl just
before serving. Should be very slushy. Very good
served in extremely hot weather. It is sweet and
you may wish to adjust sugar to your taste.

Serves 32

Fresh Mint Tea

13 tea bags
1/4 cup fresh mint leaves,
    lightly packed
Water
Juice from 2 freshly squeezed lemons
6 ounces frozen orange juice concentrate
1 cup sugar
Mint sprigs for garnish

Combine tea, mint leaves and 1 quart water in large saucepan. Cover, bring to boil and immediately remove from heat. Let steep 30 minutes. Add lemon juice, orange juice concentrate, sugar and additional water to make 2 quarts of liquid. Strain and chill. Serve over ice and garnish with mint sprigs.

Makes 2 quarts

Tea for 50

1 1/2 cups water
4 cups sugar
6 cups pineapple juice
4 cups orange juice
1 cup lemon juice
1/2 gallon weak tea
1 large bottle ginger ale
Fresh mint

Make syrup of water and sugar. Cool and add juices to tea. Just before serving add ginger ale. Serve over ice in tall glasses. Garnish with fresh mint.

From "Toots" DuBois Smith

Spiced Lemonade

Spiced syrup:
4 cups sugar
Water as needed
6 cinnamon sticks
3 cups lemon juice
6 lemons, sliced
Whole cloves as needed

In a saucepan, combine sugar, 2 cups water and cinnamon. Bring to boiling point. Reduce heat and simmer for 10 minutes. Cool. In a large container, combine spiced syrup with 2 gallons cold water and lemon juice. Chill thoroughly. Serve with sliced lemons studded with cloves.

Makes 2 1/2 gallons

Tomato Juice Cocktail

16 ounces tomato juice
1 small onion, chopped
1 garlic bud, chopped
2 peppercorns, cracked
2 tablespoons Worcestershire sauce
1 teaspoon salt
2 teaspoons sugar
2 tablespoons catsup
1/2 cup orange juice

Combine all ingredients except orange juice. Boil for 5 minutes. Strain and add orange juice. Chill to serve.

Eloise Habacker's Eggnog

8 egg yolks
1 pint whiskey
1 1/2 cups granulated sugar
1 1/2 pints whipping cream

Beat egg yolks until very light. Add whiskey slowly. Set in cold place overnight. Put sugar in another bowl, pour 1/2 pint of cream over it and also set in cold place overnight. The next morning, stir cream and sugar mixture into eggs and whiskey. Add remaining pint of cream which has been beaten fairly stiff.

Breads & Brunch

Owen-Sanderson House

Joyce's Apricot Tea Bread

3/4 cup dried apricots, chopped
1/4 cup chopped walnuts
1 1/4 cups sifted all purpose flour
1 teaspoon baking powder
1/2 teaspoon salt
1/2 teaspoon soda
1/3 cup shortening
2/3 cup sugar
2 eggs
1/2 cup buttermilk, divided
1 cup mashed ripe banana
1 cup All-Bran

Coat a 9x5" loaf pan with shortening; dust lightly
with flour and set aside. Combine chopped apricots
with walnuts and set aside. Sift dry ingredients
twice and set aside. Cream shortening with electric mixer. Slowly add sugar, a tablespoon at a
time, beating on medium speed. Add eggs one at a
time, beating between additions. Stir 1/4 cup buttermilk with mashed bananas; add All-Bran, stirring to combine. Add dry ingredients, apricots and
nuts, banana mixture and rest of buttermilk into
shortening-egg mixture. Stir just to combine.
Pour into prepared pan and bake in 325° oven 50
to 55 minutes or until wooden pick inserted in
middle comes out clean.

Maui Mango Bread

3/4 cup butter
1 1/4 cups sugar
3 eggs
1 teaspoon vanilla
1/4 teaspoon coconut extract
2 cups flour
1/2 teaspoon salt
2 teaspoons soda
1 teaspoon cinnamon
1/2 cup walnuts, chopped
2 cups mango fruit, diced with pulp
    (2 to 3 large mangoes)

Cream butter and sugar. Add 2 eggs one at a time. With third egg add vanilla and coconut extract. Add half the flour, salt, soda and cinnamon. Stir with spatula. Add remaining flour, nuts and mango. Mix well. Pour into greased and floured pan. Bake at 350° for 50 to 60 minutes.

*T*his was served to us for breakfast at Cedarberry B & B along with fresh grilled trout, fried potatoes, fresh fruits and melons, topped off with lots of warm friendship. Note: Buy mangoes when they are overripe and price reduced. Prepare and freeze in 2 cup measures for each recipe.

Rhubarb Bread

2 1/2 cups flour
1 teaspoon soda
3/4 teaspoon salt
3/4 cups butter
1 1/2 cups brown sugar, packed
1 egg
1 teaspoon lemon extract
2 teaspoons lemon rind, grated
1 cup buttermilk
1 1/2 cups fresh rhubarb, finely diced
3/4 to 1 cup pecans, chopped
1 tablespoon butter, melted
1/2 cup sugar

Sift flour, soda and salt; set aside. Cream butter and add brown sugar gradually, beating until light and fluffy. Add egg and beat well. Stir in extract and rind. Add dry ingredients alternately with buttermilk, mixing well after each addition. Stir in rhubarb and nuts. Pour batter into lightly greased bundt pan or two 8x4x2-inch loaf pans. Combine butter and sugar and sprinkle over top of batter. Bake at 325° for 1 hour and 10 minutes (less for smaller loaf pans.) Freezes well.

Blueberry Gingerbread

1/2 cup oil
1 cup sugar
1/2 teaspoon salt
3 tablespoons molasses
1 egg
2 cups flour
1/2 teaspoon ginger
1 teaspoon cinnamon
1/2 teaspoon nutmeg
1 teaspoon soda
1 cup blueberries
1 cup buttermilk
2 tablespoons sugar

Beat together oil, sugar, salt and molasses. Beat in egg. Sift together flour, ginger, cinnamon, nutmeg and soda. Dredge blueberries with a bit of flour mixture. Add rest of flour mixture to molasses mixture alternately with buttermilk, beating after each addition. Stir in blueberries. Pour into greased and floured 12x7" baking dish. Sprinkle top with 2 tablespoons sugar. Bake at 325° for 35 to 40 minutes. Cut gingerbread into squares and serve warm with butter, or serve with whipped cream as a dessert.

Quick Banana Ginger Bread

3 medium extra ripe bananas
1/2 cup brown sugar, packed
1/4 cup butter softened
3 tablespoons light molasses
1 egg
1 teaspoon vanilla
2 1/4 cups flour
1 teaspoon baking powder
1 teaspoon ground ginger
1/2 teaspoon baking soda
1/2 teaspoon salt
1 cup raisins

Slice bananas into blender and puree, (about 1 1/4 cups). With a mixer, cream sugar, butter and molasses until well blended. Beat in egg, vanilla and then bananas. Sift dry ingredients together and gradually add to banana mixture, mixing well. Stir in raisins. Pour into greased 9x5" loaf pan. Bake at 325° for 50 to 60 minutes. Cool in pan 10 minutes and turn onto wire rack to complete cooling.

Zucchini Bread

3 eggs
1 cup oil
2 cups granulated sugar
1 tablespoon vanilla
3 cups flour
1 teaspoon salt
1/4 teaspoon baking powder
1 teaspoon soda
1 tablespoon cinnamon
2 cups zucchini, peeled and grated
1/2 cup pecans, chopped

Beat eggs, oil, sugar and vanilla together. Sift flour with salt, soda, baking powder and cinnamon. Add to egg mixture and beat well. Fold in zucchini and nuts. Pour batter into two greased loaf pans. Bake at 325° for 1 hour.

In the summer when zucchini is so plentiful, it can be grated and frozen for baking later. A delicious bread served at breakfast, snack time or with a meal. It is also good spread with cream cheese.

Burwell's "Desperation" Corn Bread

1/4 stick butter
3 eggs
1/2 cup corn meal
1/2 cup whole wheat flour
2 cups milk
2 teaspoons baking soda
Salt

Preheat oven to 325°. Melt butter and place in mixing bowl. Add pinch of salt. Add eggs and mix thoroughly. Stir in corn meal and whole wheat flour. Mix in milk and baking soda. Pour into a buttered and floured pie plate, stirring while pouring to keep mixture consistently distributed. Bake for 45 minutes. Sweetener, like maple syrup, may be added for taste.

Special Cornbread

1 stick butter
8 ounces sour cream
8-ounce can cream style corn
2 teaspoons sugar
2 eggs, beaten
1 cup self-rising cornmeal

Melt butter in iron skillet. Stir in sour cream, corn, sugar, eggs, and cornmeal. Place skillet with mixture in 400° oven and bake 20 to 25 minutes. Do not use corn bread mix!

Serves 6 to 8

Connie McClain's Corn Light Bread

4 cups self-rising cornmeal
1 cup plain flour
1 1/2 cups sugar
2 teaspoons salt
1 teaspoon baking soda
1/2 cup vegetable oil
4 cups sour milk or buttermilk*

Mix all dry ingredients together in a large bowl.
Add liquid ingredients and stir until blended well.
Spray 2 loaf pans with vegetable spray and divide
batter into each. Bake at 325° until breaks away
from side of pan. Remove from pans while hot and
immediately wrap loosely in waxpaper. This will
steam loaves. When cool, wrap tightly.

*In a 4 cup measure place 2/3 cup vinegar and add
sweet milk to the top of measure and stir. This
works better than sour milk or buttermilk.

Makes 2 loaves

Freezes well and can be cooked in an angel
food cake pan.

Southern Spoon Bread

1 cup cornmeal
3 cups sweet milk
1 teaspoon salt
1 teaspoon baking powder
2 tablespoons salad oil
   or melted shortening
3 well beaten egg yolks
3 stiffly beaten egg whites

Cook cornmeal and 2 cups milk until the consistency of mush. Remove from heat; add salt, baking powder, salad oil and 1 cup milk. Stir in egg yolks, fold in egg whites. Bake in greased 2-quart baking dish at 325° for 1 hour or until mixture doesn't adhere to knife. Serve immediately.

Serves 6

Feather Light Biscuits

2 cups flour
1 tablespoon sugar
1 teaspoon salt
1 tablespoon baking powder
Shortening, the size of a large egg
1 cake yeast
1/4 cup lukewarm water
3/4 cup milk

Sift together flour, sugar, salt and baking powder.
Cut in shortening. Dissolve yeast cake in water;
add milk. Add yeast, water and milk to dry mixture. Knead well; let rise about 20 minutes.
Roll out biscuits and place in refrigerator. Take
out as needed and let rise about 10 minutes. Bake
at 400° until brown.

A cruet of grape juice, placed on a dinner table,
allows everyone to add some to their glasses of iced
tea.

Freeze Biscuits

1/4 cup shortening
2 cups sifted self-rising flour
2/3 cup cold milk

Cut shortening into flour until particles are like coarse meal. Stir in milk to make a soft dough. Turn dough out on lightly floured board or cloth; knead until smooth. Roll dough out and cut with floured cutter. Place on ungreased baking sheet; brush tops lightly with milk and put in freezer.

When frozen hard, about 1 hour, remove and put in a plastic bag. When ready to use, remove from freezer and place on ungreased baking sheet. Bake in preheated 450° oven for 12 to 15 minutes.

Note: Do not let biscuits thaw before baking and be sure oven temperature has reached 450°.

Applesauce Oat Muffins

1 1/2 cups uncooked rolled oats
1 1/4 cups all purpose
    whole-grain flour
2 teaspoons cinnamon
1 teaspoon baking powder
3/4 teaspoon low-sodium baking soda
1 cup unsweetened applesauce
1/3 cup honey
1/3 cup vegetable oil
1 egg white
1 teaspoon vanilla
1/4 cup chopped nuts

Heat oven to 325°. Line a muffin tray with paper baking cups. Combine oats, flour, cinnamon, baking powder and baking soda. Add applesauce, honey, oil, egg white and vanilla; mix well. Stir in nuts. Fill muffin cups; bake 25 to 30 minutes or until golden brown.

Makes 12 muffins

Norma's Bacon

Medium to thick sliced bacon
Milk
Flour (plain or self-rising)

Dip bacon slices into milk, then into flour. Place on cookie sheet sprayed with Pam. Bake at 325° until brown and crispy. Drain on paper towels.

Very good served as a meat with fresh vegetables in the summer. Also, makes good bacon and tomato sandwiches. Does not shrink.

Optional: Season with black pepper.

Breakfast Casserole

8 ounces dried beef
6 ounces sliced mushrooms
1/2 cup margarine
1/2 cup flour
Pepper to taste
1 quart milk
16 eggs
1/2 teaspoon salt
1 small can evaporated milk
1/4 cup margarine

Tear dried beef into manageable pieces, but not too small. Drain mushrooms, reserving liquid. Heat margarine in large saucepan; add dried beef and mushrooms. Heat, stirring until well coated. Sprinkle with flour and pepper; heat, stirring until slightly crisped. Add milk and mushroom liquid; cook, stirring briskly until smooth and slightly thickened. Grease a 3-quart casserole. Beat eggs; stir in salt and evaporated milk. Melt margarine in large skillet; add egg mixture. Cook very slowly, stirring constantly until thickened but not firm. Pour into greased casserole. Bake at 325° for approximately 35 minutes or until firm to the touch.

Breakfast Pork Maple Pie

6 large tart cooking apples
1 cup light brown sugar
2 tablespoons flour
1/2 teaspoon black pepper,
    freshly ground
1 teaspoon cinnamon
Pinch of ground ginger
1/2 pound thick sliced bacon, diced
Pastry for two crust 9" pie

Peel, core and thinly slice apples. Mix flour, sugar and spices. Combine with apples and arrange in prepared 9" pie pan. Sprinkle with bacon. Top with remaining pastry, seal and flute edges, cut vents. Brush top with beaten egg mixed with water and sprinkle with poppy seed. Bake in preheated 450° oven for 10 minutes; reduce heat to 325° and bake for 1 1/4 hours longer.

Leftover bits of country ham or baked ham can be substituted for bacon.

Delicious served by itself or very good with scrambled eggs and sliced tomatoes.

Daus Brown Haus All in One Quiche

1 1/2 cups milk
1/2 cup biscuit mix
6 tablespoons butter,
　room temperature
3 eggs
Pinch of salt
1 cup diced ham, turkey, shrimp,
　chicken, bacon or vegetables
2 green onions, chopped
1 4-ounce can sliced mushrooms,
　drained
1 cup grated sharp cheddar cheese

Preheat oven to 350°. Combine first five ingredients in blender and mix well. Turn into ungreased deep dish 9-inch or regular 10-inch pan. Add meat, shellfish, or vegetables, poking into batter. Top with onions, mushrooms and cheese. Bake until top is golden brown, about 45 minutes. Let stand 10 minutes before serving.

Serves 6

Cheese and Sausage Grits Casserole

2 cups boiling water
1 cup instant grits
1 pound bulk sausage,
    sautéed and drained
1 cup cheddar cheese, grated
1/4 cup butter melted
2 large eggs, beaten
1/2 teaspoon granulated garlic
1/2 teaspoon salt
1/8 teaspoon black pepper
8-ounce can mild green chilies, diced
Dash of Tabasco (optional)

Combine grits and boiling water. Add sausage, cheese and remaining ingredients. Mix and pour into buttered 9x13-inch baking dish. Bake at 325° for 1 hour.

Serves 10

Uncommonly Good
Sausage and Cheese Strata

4 cups dry bread cubes or crumbs
1 pound bulk sausage,
    browned and drained
1/2 cup green pepper, minced
1 cup green onions, sliced
8 eggs, beaten
4 cups milk
1 pound sharp cheddar cheese, grated
2 teaspoons ground mustard
1/2 teaspoon Worcestershire sauce
1/4 teaspoon paprika
8 bacon slices, fried crisp,
    drained and crumbled

Spray 9x13" baking dish. Sprinkle bread cubes evenly over bottom. Sprinkle cooked sausage over crumbs. Place pepper and onions over sausage. Mix eggs, milk, cheese, mustard, Worcestershire and paprika. Pour over sausage. Sprinkle bacon over top. Cover and refrigerate overnight. Bake uncovered at 350° for 50 to 60 minutes.

Serves 12 to 15

Uncommonly good Strata from my good friend Joyce, whom I met in Seaside, Oregon at James Beard's cooking class. She and her husband, Mick, have retired and now run a Bed and Breakfast Inn in Cedaredge, Colorado. It is worth the trip just to sample her "goodies".

Creole Eggs Curtis Lee

1 medium size onion, chopped fine
2 tablespoons bacon fat
1 15-ounce can tomatoes
Salt and pepper to taste
Dash Tabasco sauce
1/2 cup butter
3 tablespoons flour, heaping
1 cup milk
8 large hard boiled eggs
1 cup toasted crumbs

Sauté onions in bacon fat. Add tomatoes and
simmer until onions are well done. Add salt,
Tabasco and pepper to taste. This mixture should
be highly seasoned. Make a white sauce of 1/2
the butter, all the flour and milk. Sauce should
be thick. Add tomato mixture to white sauce and
stir well. Slice eggs into well buttered casserole,
pour tomato mixture over eggs. Mix bread
crumbs with remaining butter, and sprinkle on
top. Bake at 325° until crumbs are brown.
(Chopped bell peppers may be added with onions if
you like.)

Serves 6 to 8

Egg Croquettes

3 tablespoons butter
3 tablespoons flour
3/4 teaspoon salt
1/4 teaspoon pepper
Dash paprika
3/4 cup milk
1 cup whole-kernel corn,
    cooked and drained
1 teaspoon parsley, chopped
1/2 cup bread crumbs
3 hard cooked eggs, chopped

Melt butter; add flour, salt, pepper and a little paprika. Add milk and cook until smooth and thick. Remove from heat and add other ingredients except bread crumbs and chopped eggs. Shape into croquettes. Roll in crumbs, then eggs, then crumbs again. Fry in hot fat.

Hot Mushroom Sandwiches

8 slices thick bread
   (use loaf of Italian or French bread
   and cut into slices at least
   3/4 inch thick)
Soft butter
16 thin slices tomato
2 cups mushrooms, thinly sliced
Black pepper, coarsely ground

Parmesan Topping

1 cup mayonnaise
1/2 teaspoon lemon peel, grated
1 tablespoon chives, chopped
1 tablespoon lemon juice
1/2 cup Parmesan cheese, grated

Lightly spread both sides of bread with butter.
Place on broiler pan 4 to 5 inches from heat.
Toast lightly on both sides. When second side is
done, top each with two tomato slices, 1/4 cup
mushrooms and sprinkling of pepper. Spread each
with a generous spoon of Parmesan topping.
Return to broiler and broil about 3 minutes, or
until bubbly and lightly browned.
Serve immediately.

Serve with shrimp salad on avocado half on bed of greens.
Garnish with ripe olives and carrot sticks.

Serves 8

Apple and Cheddar Gratin

2 pounds Granny Smith apples, peeled,
   cored and cut into 1/4" slices
1/2 cup raisins
1/2 teaspoon cinnamon
1/4 cup fresh lemon juice
3/4 cup brown sugar, firmly packed
1/2 cup flour
1/8 teaspoon salt
1/2 stick cold unsalted butter,
   cut into squares
1 cup finely grated extra
   sharp cheddar cheese

In a well buttered 1-quart shallow baking dish,
arrange apple slices and sprinkle with raisins,
cinnamon and lemon juice. In a small bowl combine sugar, flour and salt. Blend in butter until
mixture resembles coarse meal, then add cheese
and toss. Sprinkle mixture over apples and bake
in the upper third of oven, preheated at 325° for
30 minutes, or until apples are tender. Serve
the gratin as a dessert or as an accompaniment
to roast pork or ham.

Serves 4 to 6

Frances Williams' Scalloped Rhubarb

3 cups stale bread, cubed
1 stick butter, melted
2 cups uncooked rhubarb, diced
  (I use frozen)
1 cup sugar
4 teaspoons water

Combine all ingredients, mixing well. Place in a buttered oblong pan. Put one teaspoon water in each corner of pan. Bake at 325 for 45 minutes.

Serves 6

Cheese Soufflé

1 level tablespoon butter
1 level tablespoon flour
1 cup grated cheese
1 cup milk
Salt
Pepper
3 eggs, separated

Put butter and flour together in pan; stir on low heat until blended without browning. Add the grated cheese, milk, salt and pepper. Set aside to cool. Beat whites and yolks separately, then add mixture in saucepan to beaten egg yolks and blend thoroughly. Fold in whites stiffly beaten; turn the soufflé into a well greased pan or dish. Bake in a moderate oven about 25 minutes.
Serve immediately or it may fall.

Do not think because you have made soufflés before you can improve on this — go implicitly by this recipe and it will be absolutely perfect.

Soups

Vaughan-Lynch House

Linda's Asparagus Leek Chowder

3 cups sliced fresh mushrooms
3 large leeks,
   sliced diagonally in 3/4 inch length,
   using 1/2 way up leek
10-ounce package frozen asparagus
6 tablespoons butter
1/2 teaspoon salt
Dash pepper
3 tablespoons flour
2 cups rich chicken stock
2 cups half and half cream
12-ounce can white corn or hominy
1 tablespoon chopped pimento

In large saucepan cook mushrooms, leeks and asparagus in butter until tender, but not browned, about 10 minutes. Stir in salt, pepper and flour. Add chicken broth and half and half. Cook until thick and creamy, stirring constantly. Do not let boil. Add corn or hominy and pimento. Correct seasonings.

Serves 6 to 8

Cream of Avocado Soup

2 large avocados
1/2 teaspoon salt
1 cup half and half
2 teaspoons lemon juice
2 cups rich chicken broth
1/4 cup dry sherry
Lime or sour cream

Cut the avocados in half. Remove the seeds and scoop out the flesh. Place the avocado flesh, salt, half and half, and lemon juice in a blender of food processor. Blend to a smooth puree. Pour puree into a pan or bowl. Heat chicken broth to boiling. Slowly add hot broth to puree. Add sherry. May be served hot or cold.

If serving hot, heat, but do not boil! If serving cold, refrigerate for several hours and serve in cold cups or bowls. Garnish with a thin slice of lime or a dollop of sour cream.

Serves 6 to 8 as a first course

Beer Cheese Soup

2 cloves garlic, minced
2 tablespoons Schmaltz or butter
4 cups rich chicken stock, fat removed
1/2 cup flour
1 can beer
1 pound sharp cheddar cheese, grated
1 teaspoon Lawrey's Seasoned salt
1/2 teaspoon black pepper,
   freshly ground
1/8 teaspoon cayenne pepper

In heavy saucepan, sauté garlic in Schmaltz or butter. Over medium heat, add chicken stock and bring to a boil. Stir in flour that has been whisked in beer. Cook until slightly thickened, stirring constantly. Add grated cheese and seasonings; stir constantly until cheese has melted.

Serves 6

Cheesy Chicken Chowder

1 cup carrot, shredded
1/4 cup onion, chopped
4 tablespoons butter
1/4 cup flour
2 cups milk
13-ounce can chicken broth
1 cup cooked chicken, diced
2 tablespoons dry white wine
1/2 teaspoon celery seed
1/2 teaspoon Worcestershire sauce
1 cup sharp cheese, shredded

In a heavy saucepan, sauté carrot and onion in butter until tender but not brown. Blend in flour, milk and broth. Stir constantly until thickened and bubbly. Stir in chicken, wine, celery seed and Worcestershire sauce. Add the grated cheese and stir until thickened. Season to taste.

Serves 4 or 5

Broccoli Soup

1 1/2 tablespoons chicken stock
1/4 teaspoon white pepper
1/8 cup parsley flakes
3/4 teaspoon lemon juice
1/3 cup diced celery
2 pints milk
2 pints half and half
1 quart fresh broccoli
1/8 pound butter
1/3 cup flour
1/4 cup sherry

Cook first 7 ingredients over low heat, stirring occasionally. Clean and cut broccoli; boil for 12 minutes, until tender. Add immediately to mixture. Increase heat to medium high; simmer and stir. Melt butter, add flour; stir into soup. When soup thickens, add sherry. Mix well.

Bunny's Pumpkin Soup

2 tablespoons butter
2 ribs celery, chopped
2 onions, chopped
2 cups cooked pumpkin, mashed
4 cups chicken or beef stock,
   or combination of both
1 bay leaf
1 teaspoon dried basil
1 teaspoon dried thyme
1 cup heavy cream
Sour cream

Melt butter in large saucepan. Sauté celery and onions in butter until transparent. Add pumpkin, stock and spices. Simmer over low heat 30 minutes to one hour, stirring often. Just before serving, stir in cream and reheat. Do not let boil. Soup can be served without adding cream. Add dollop of sour cream to each bowl.

An original recipe from my friend Bunny, who has many originals.

Dusty's
Red Mushroom Soup

1 pound fresh mushrooms, sliced
1 onion, chopped
2 cloves garlic, minced
1 tablespoon olive oil
1 tablespoon butter
3 tablespoons tomato paste
3 cups chicken broth
Sweet vermouth to taste

Sauté mushrooms, onion and garlic in olive oil and butter. Add remaining ingredients and simmer for about 10 minutes. Pour into bowls and dust with Parmesan cheese.

Serves 2 to 4

Potato Soup

6 cups diced potatoes
Juice of 1 lemon
Water to cover
1 large white onion, diced
3 to 4 cups carrots, diced
1 stalk celery, chopped
1/4 cup butter
Salt and Pepper to taste
1 tablespoon parsley
1 tablespoon chives
Small bay leaf
1 quart chicken broth
4 tablespoons flour
2 cups whipping cream
6 ounces sour cream

Place potatoes, lemon juice and water in large saucepan. Cook for 30 minutes. Sauté onion, carrots and celery in butter. Drain potatoes, add onion mixture. Season with salt, pepper, parsley, chives and bay leaf. Add chicken broth. Cook 1/2 hour. Blend flour into whipping cream. Mix into potato mixture and simmer no more than 30 minutes. Add sour cream and blend.

This soup freezes well so may be prepared a few days ahead of serving.

Okra and Tomato Gumbo

1/4 cup vegetable oil
1/2 cup green pepper, chopped
1/4 cup onion, chopped
1/4 cup celery, chopped
1/4 cup flour
4 cups chicken stock
3/4 pound okra, cut in 1 inch pieces
1/8 teaspoon cayenne pepper
6 drops Tabasco
1/2 teaspoon thyme
6 tomatoes, peeled and diced
2 cups cooked rice
1 tablespoon cilantro leaves

Sauté green pepper, onion and celery in oil. Slowly stir in flour. Add chicken stock gradually, stirring constantly. Add remaining ingredients except rice and cilantro. Simmer until vegetables are tender. Add rice and cilantro.

Serves 8 to 10

Garden Vegetable Soup

1/2 cup chopped onion
1/2 cup chopped celery
2 tablespoons oil
4 cups chicken broth
4 large tomatoes,
    peeled and chopped (4 cups)
1 1/2 cups green beans,
    cut into 1/2" pieces
1 large carrot, sliced
1 tablespoon chopped fresh basil
    or 1 teaspoon, dried
1 teaspoon sugar
1 bay leaf, crumbled
2 medium zucchini, sliced
1 1/2 cups sliced okra
1 cup corn
Salt and pepper to taste

In large saucepan sauté onion and celery in oil
until tender. Add broth, tomatoes, beans, carrots,
basil, sugar and bay leaf. Bring to boil; reduce
heat, cover and simmer 30 minutes. Add remaining ingredients, return to boil; simmer covered five
minutes or until tender. Can be served as main
dish with bowls of leftover chopped meats, shredded
cheese, dumplings or pasta and let each person
choose what to add.

Succotash Soup

1/2 stick of butter
1 medium size onion, chopped
1/2 teaspoon curry powder
Salt and pepper to taste
8 3/4-ounce can cream style corn
Two 10 1/2-ounce cans oyster stew
16-ounce can Italian tomatoes
8 ounces sour cream

Melt butter, add chopped onion, cook over low heat until transparent. Add curry powder, salt and pepper; heat and mix well. Chop and add all the other ingredients; mix well and heat. This is better if made the day before serving. Serve hot or cold.

6 to 8 cups

Imy's Zucchini Soup

1/2 pound ground beef or turkey
1 medium onion
2 to 3 small zucchini, thinly sliced
1 can tomatoes
1 can water
1 cup pasta
3/4 pound mild
    Mexican Style Velveeta, cubed

Sauté ground beef or turkey and onion. Add zucchini, tomatoes, water and pasta. Cook about 12 minutes. Add Velvetta.

Did you know.....

Trimming fat off meat before cooking is better than trimming it after? (Meat absorbs fat during cooking.)

Most of an egg's cholesterol is in the yolk while most of the protein is in the white?

Canned beans may have as much as 40 times more sodium than home-cooked beans?

You should be wary of "Dieter's Special Platters" in restaurants? The hamburgers and cottage cheese they usually feature are loaded with saturated fat.

Peanut Butter Soup

3 ounces minced onions
3 ounces minced celery
3 ounces butter
1 tablespoon flour
4 cups rich chicken stock
8 ounces peanut butter
1 cup half and half, heated
1 teaspoon salt
1/4 teaspoon black pepper

Lightly sauté onions and celery in butter. While stirring, add flour, chicken stock, peanut butter, half and half, salt and pepper. Simmer about 15 minutes. If too thick, thin to proper consistency with milk. Garnish with bacon crumbs or minced country ham.

Serves 6

Orr's Chili Parlor Chili

2 pounds extra lean ground beef
1 quart water
4 small onions, chopped
1 teaspoon garlic powder
4 teaspoons chili powder
1 teaspoon cinnamon
2 teaspoons crushed red pepper
4 teaspoons cumin
1 tablespoon salt
5 bay leaves
1 teaspoon ground allspice
1 1/2 tablespoons vinegar
2 tablespoons Worcestershire sauce
6-ounce can tomato paste

In a four quart pot, add ground beef, bit by bit to boiling water and stir until beef separates to a fine texture. Add remaining ingredients stirring to blend. Bring to a boil; reduce heat and simmer, uncovered, for about 3 hours. Last hour, pot may be covered once desired consistency is reached.

Note: Place bay leaves in tea ball for easy removal.

Makes 4 generous servings if meat sauce is spooned over spaghetti, kidney beans or rice.

Spiked Lobster Soup

1 can cream of mushroom soup
1 can chicken soup with rice
1 large can evaporated milk
2 ounces lobster or crab meat,
    fresh or frozen
1/4 cup bourbon or sherry

Stir together soups and milk. Add lobster or crab meat. At the last minute, stir in bourbon or sherry.

This soup can be made ahead of time, but the liquor must be added at the last minute.

Cold Chocolate Fruit Soup

6-ounce package semi-sweet
  chocolate chips
1 cup milk
10-ounce package frozen strawberries,
  drained
1 banana, sliced
1 1/4 cups heavy cream
1/2 teaspoon vanilla
1/2 teaspoon cinnamon
Whipped cream or sour cream, optional

In small saucepan, place 1/2 package chocolate chips with milk and melt over low heat. Combine with remaining ingredients and blend until smooth. Chill until ready to serve. Place second half of chocolate chips in dry blender and chop into small particles; set aside. When ready to serve, garnish with whipped cream or sour cream and chopped chocolate morsels.

Note: Morsel-milk mixture will contain flecks of chocolate. This will not be a smooth mixture.

Serves 6

It was quite difficult introducing cold soups to the general public. Now they are a favorite. This particular one can also be used as a dessert soup.

Cucumber Soup

1 cup sour cream
1 cucumber, peeled, seeded and sliced
1/4 teaspoon dry mustard
1/2 teaspoon instant chicken bouillon
1 tablespoon snipped chives or
1 green onion
Salt and pepper to taste

Put all ingredients into a blender and blend only until cucumber is finely chopped, not smooth. Chill and serve. Garnish with a sprinkle of dill or chives, if desired.

Serves 2 to 4

When Jean and I were cooking at the Ninth Street House and we had all the pots and pans soiled and stacked to the ceiling, we would look at each and say "I'm really cooking!"

Gazpacho Soup

2 14 1/2-ounce cans stewed tomatoes
1 cup cucumber, peeled and diced
1 cup green pepper, chopped
1 clove garlic
2 tablespoons chives
2 tablespoons parsley
2 tablespoons basil
2 tablespoons tarragon
1 cup clear beef stock or consommé
1 tablespoon Worcestershire sauce
6 drops Tabasco sauce
6 twists of ground black pepper
Salt to taste

Put into blender or food processor and liquefy.
For garnish add fresh tomato, diced cucumber, diced
green pepper and/or toasted croutons. Serve soup
very cold; pass garnish separately.

Serves 6

Cold Peach Soup

1 cup water
1/4 cup sugar
1 teaspoon whole cloves
1 cinnamon stick
1 1/2 teaspoons arrowroot
    (or cornstarch) dissolved in
2 cups dry white wine
2 1/2 pounds fresh peaches or frozen,
    defrosted and undrained peaches,
    pureed

As a dessert

Pound cake
1/2 cup whipping cream
2 tablespoons powdered sugar
1/2 cup sour cream
1 cup blueberries, rinsed and drained

Combine first 4 ingredients in a medium saucepan and bring to boil over medium-high heat. Reduce heat, cover and simmer 30 minutes; strain and return to pan. Add arrowroot and wine mixture and blend thoroughly. Bring to boil, stirring occa-

sionally. Let cool, then add pureed peaches; mix well. Ladle into soup bowls and serve as a first course.

To serve as a dessert, spoon over thick slices of pound cake and garnish.

For garnish: Whip cream with sugar in chilled bowl until it holds peaks. Fold in sour cream and blueberries; chill thoroughly.

This is our recipe as it appeared in Bon Appetit's 1981 Favorite Restaurant Recipes.

Cold Watercress Soup

2 bunches watercress, leaves only
2 small zucchini, sliced
2 leeks
1 large potato, peeled and sliced
1 small head butter lettuce
2 scallions
1/2 cup parsley leaves
1 tablespoon chicken bouillon granules
2 cups water
1 cup whipping cream
Sour cream or sherry, optional

Slice all vegetables. Simmer in bouillon granules
and water until tender, 20 to 30 minutes. Puree
in food processor and return to pot. Add whipping
cream and season to taste. Chill.

If desired, place dollop of sour cream or a tablespoon of sherry in each soup bowl.

Serves 6 to 8 as a first course

Salads
&
Dressings

Alben Barkley Museum

Jo's Jellied Potato Salad

5 cups diced cooked potatoes
1 tablespoon vinegar
2 teaspoons salt
1 cup chopped onion
1 teaspoon celery seed
1 1/2 cups mayonnaise or salad dressing
2 small packages lemon gelatin
2 1/2 cups boiling water
1/4 cup vinegar
1/4 cup cold water
9 green pepper rings
9 red pepper rings or pimento strips
1 cup diced cucumbers

Sprinkle potatoes with vinegar and salt. Toss with onion, celery seed and salad dressing; chill. Meanwhile dissolve gelatin in boiling water. Add vinegar. Reserve 1 1/3 cups of this mixture. Add cold water to remaining mixture. Pour into 9x9x2-inch pan. Chill until slightly thick. Arrange green and red pepper rings in gelatin. Chill until set. Chill remaining gelatin until partially set, then beat until soft peaks form. Fold in potato salad and cucumbers. Spoon over gelatin in pan, chill until set. Invert to unmold and cut into squares.

Serves 9

Avocado Surprise

2 large ripe avocados
Lemon juice, fresh or bottled
Lettuce leaves

Filling
2 cups cooked chicken, diced
1 cup orange sections
1/2 cup green grapes, cut in half
1/4 cup walnuts or pecans, chopped
1/4 cup onion, finely chopped

Dressing
5 tablespoons olive oil
2 tablespoons lemon juice
2 tablespoons parsley, chopped
2 teaspoons dried basil
Salt and pepper

At serving time, cut avocados in half lengthwise.
Peel and brush with lemon juice. Combine filling
ingredients and chill for 1 hour. Mix dressing
ingredients in jar. Mix filling and dressing (shake
dressing well first) and heap on avocado halves.
Arrange on bed of lettuce leaves.

Note: For elegant, alfresco summer lunches the avocado is a
savory kitchen quickie. Crown the nutty fruit with a scoop of
chicken salad. Serve with warm rolls and chilled Chablis.

Candy's
Chinese Cabbage Salad

1 head cabbage, shredded
1 bunch green onions, chopped
2 tablespoons slivered almonds, toasted
1 tablespoons sesame seeds, toasted
1/2 cup oil
1/4 cup vinegar
2 tablespoons sugar
1 teaspoon salt
1 teaspoon Accent
1/2 teaspoon pepper
2 chicken breasts, boiled and chopped
2 packages ramen noodles, crumbled

Combine cabbage, green onion, almonds and sesame seeds. Mix oil, vinegar, sugar, salt, Accent, pepper and chicken. Toss with salad ingredients. Add noodles and toss again right before serving.

Serves 8 to 10

Dottie's Spinach Salad

10-ounce package fresh spinach,
  washed, drained and torn
12-ounce carton cottage cheese, rinsed
1/2 cup pecans, chopped
1/2 cup sour cream
1/4 cup sugar
2 tablespoons vinegar
2 tablespoons horseradish
1/2 teaspoon dry mustard
1/4 teaspoon salt

Combine spinach, cottage cheese and pecans into large serving bowl. Mix together remaining ingredients for dressing, then combine with spinach mixture.

Serves 4

Frances Williams' Garden Salad

1 tomato soup can filled with water
1/2 cup vinegar
1 cup sugar
2 small boxes raspberry jello
1 package unflavored gelatin,
    dissolved as directed
2 cans tomato soup
1 green pepper, chopped
2 cups grated cabbage
1 chopped onion
1 cup chopped celery
Dash black pepper
Salt to taste

Topping
4 ounces cream cheese
2 tablespoons salad dressing

Bring water, vinegar and sugar to a boil. Add jello and gelatin and let cool. Add tomato soup, then mix with vegetables and seasonings. Refrigerate overnight.

Prepare topping by mixing cream cheese with salad dressing. Spread over salad.

Serves 12

Joyce's Spinach Rice Salad

1 1/3 cups water
2/3 cup long grain rice
1 teaspoon lemon juice
1/2 teaspoon salt
1/2 bay leaf
1/2 cup Italian dressing
2 cups fresh spinach leaves, chopped
1/3 cup diced pepper
1/3 cup frozen peas, defrosted
2 tablespoons parsley, snipped
2 green onions, finely chopped
2-ounce jar pimento, chopped
1 medium tomato, seeded and cubed
4 slices bacon, cooked,
    drained and crumbled

Bring water to a boil. Add rice, lemon juice, salt
and bay leaf. Cover and reduce heat to warm.
Steam rice until all moisture is absorbed. Remove
bay leaf and toss with 1/4 cup dressing.
Refrigerate until chilled. Add remaining salad
dressing and ingredients except bacon. Correct seasonings, then cover and chill. At serving time, mix
in crumbled bacon and serve in clear glass bowl.

Serves 6 to 8

Good hot weather salad! This was served to us on a picnic in
Aspen, Colorado.

Pickled Beet Salad

2 bunches red beets, trimmed
Salt
2 tablespoons red wine vinegar
2 tablespoons oil, vegetable or olive
1 teaspoon sugar
1/4 teaspoon ground cumin
Salt and pepper to taste
1 large red onion, thinly sliced
4 tablespoons chopped parsley

Place beets in saucepan and cover with water.
Salt to taste. Bring to a boil and simmer until
tender; let cool. Remove skin under cold running
water. Slice beets into salad bowl. Add vinegar,
oil, sugar, cumin, salt and pepper. Blend well.
Toss with onions and parsley.

Nat's Cole Slaw

1 head cabbage, chopped
2 onions, chopped
1 green pepper, chopped
2 ribs celery, chopped
1 small can pimento, drained and chopped
2 cups granulated sugar
1 cup cider vinegar
1 cup salad oil
2 teaspoons sugar
1 tablespoon salt

Combine first five ingredients and pour 2 cups
sugar on top. Boil next four ingredients and pour
hot mixture over slaw. Chill overnight.

Serves 10 to 12

Pineapple Slaw
with Blue Cheese Dressing

4 cups cabbage, shredded
1 large carrot, shredded
1/2 cup radishes, sliced
1/2 cup green pepper, slivered
1 cup pineapple tidbits, well drained
3/4 cup buttermilk
3/4 cup mayonnaise
1/3 cup blue cheese, crumbled
1/2 teaspoon celery seed

Toss together cabbage, carrot, radishes, green pepper and pineapple tidbits. Combine buttermilk, mayonnaise, blue cheese and celery seed. Pour over cabbage mixture. Cover and chill well before serving.

Serves 6 to 8

Sis Michael's
Prepare Ahead Salad

1 can cut green beans
1 package frozen broccoli cuts
  (not cooked)
1/2 head raw cauliflower
4 green onions, with tops
1 can water chestnuts, sliced
1 bottle Kraft Creamy
  Italian Dressing

Cut green beans and broccoli cuts again. Slice cauliflower and green onions into small pieces. Mix
all ingredients with dressing and refrigerate
overnight. Garnish with tomato wedges or cherry
tomatoes.

Serves 8 to 10

Mandarin Orange Salad

2 heads Romaine lettuce
1 bag spinach
1 head iceberg lettuce
3 cans mandarin oranges, drained
1 cup bacon bits
1 package sliced almonds, toasted

Wash lettuces and spinach and pat dry. Shred in large salad bowl. Add remaining ingredients. Pour dressing over when ready to serve.

Serves 10

Dressing
2 1/2 cups oil
1 1/4 cups sugar
1 1/4 cups white vinegar
3 teaspoons salt

Mix all ingredients in large jar. Shake and keep refrigerated.

Spiced Peach Salad

28-ounce jar spiced peaches
6 ounces lemon gelatin
4 oranges
1/2 cup orange juice
1/2 cup pecans, chopped and toasted
1/2 cup maraschino cherries, chopped

Drain spiced peaches, reserving juice; dice. Heat peach juice and dissolve gelatin in juice. Peel, section and chop oranges. After gelatin has partially congealed, add chopped peaches, oranges, orange juice, toasted pecans and cherries. Stir well and pour into mold that has been coated with mayonnaise.

Serves 12

Nothing went to waste when I was growing up. Even a hen that was hit by a passing car was quickly prepared, perhaps into chicken noodle soup and canned for future enjoyment.

Cranberry Fluff

2 cups raw cranberries, ground
3 cups miniature marshmallows
3/4 cup granulated sugar
2 cups tart apples, diced and unpeeled
1/2 cup grapes, cut in half
    with seeds removed
1/2 cup toasted pecans, chopped
Pinch salt
1 cup heavy cream, whipped

Combine cranberries, marshmallows and sugar. Let set overnight. Add apples, grapes, pecans, and salt. Fold together gently with whipped cream. Chill. Turn into serving bowl, or spoon into individual lettuce cups. Trim with a cluster of grapes, if desired.

Serves 8 to 10

"When my son Jay was in grade school, he told me one of his teachers, Mrs. Mathis, would like my recipe for 'Cranberry Flop'!"

Strawberry and Lettuce Salad

Leaf lettuce (green and red)
Sliced Strawberries

Dressing
3/4 cup sugar
1/2 cup red wine vinegar
1/4 cup olive oil
1 teaspoon paprika
1/2 teaspoon pepper
2 cloves garlic, minced
   (more or less to taste)

Mix lettuce and strawberries in large bowl. Mix dressing ingredients in microwave-safe bowl. Microwave on High for 1 minute to blend. May serve warm or cold over salad.

Very GOOD!

Cranberry Chutney

2 cups fresh cranberries
3/4 cup brown sugar
1/2 cup white raisins
1/2 cup chopped celery
1/2 cup chopped apple
1/2 cup water
1/4 cup coarsely chopped walnuts
2 tablespoons finely snipped ginger
2 tablespoons lemon juice
1 teaspoon onion salt
1/4 teaspoon cloves

Combine all ingredients in saucepan. Bring to boiling, stirring constantly. Simmer, uncovered, 15 minutes stirring occasionally. Store covered in refrigerator.

Makes 2 cups

Fruit Salad with Chutney

Avocado, cut into pieces
Orange, sectioned
Grapefruit, sectioned
White grapes
Major Grey's chutney
Lettuce

Arrange any portions you wish of avocado, oranges, grapefruit and grapes in lettuce cups. Pour over each serving 1 generous teaspoon chutney. Serve with French dressing.

French Dressing
1 clove garlic, crushed
1 teaspoon salt
1/2 teaspoon black pepper
1 teaspoon mustard
1 teaspoon sugar
2 pinches sweet basil
2 tablespoons vinegar
4 tablespoons olive oil

Crush garlic in bowl, mix with salt, pepper, mustard, sugar and basil (use powdered basil or powder the leaves between fingers). Add vinegar and stir. Add olive oil and combine thoroughly.

Strawberry Aspic

1 can stewed tomatoes
2 tablespoons grated onion
3 tablespoons tarragon vinegar
2 shakes of Tabasco
1/2 teaspoon salt
1 small package strawberry gelatin

Blend tomatoes and onion in blender, add vinegar,
Tabasco and salt. Bring to a full boil and stir in
gelatin. Chill in molds or glass dish.

Serves 6

Avocado Mousse

1 tablespoon unflavored gelatin
2 tablespoons cold water
3 ounces lime gelatin
2 cups hot water
1 cup ripe avocado, mashed
1/2 cup mayonnaise
1/2 cup cream, whipped

Dissolve unflavored gelatin in cold water; add top lime gelatin that has been dissolved in hot water. Stir until completely dissolved. Place in refrigerator until partially congealed. Add remaining ingredients and pour into mold that has been coated with mayonnaise. Return to refrigerator until completely congealed.

Serves 6 to 8

Ham Mousse

1 envelope unflavored gelatin
3/4 cup cold water
1 cup mayonnaise
2 cups cooked ham, chopped
1/2 cup celery, chopped
1/4 cup green pepper, chopped
1 teaspoon onion, grated
1/2 cup cream, whipped

Sprinkle gelatin over cold water in saucepan.
Place over low heat, stir until gelatin dissolves,
3 to 4 minutes. Gradually add to mayonnaise,
stirring until smooth. Chill until slightly thickened. Stir in ham, celery, pepper and onion. Fold
in whipped cream. Pour into 1 quart mold and chill
until firm. Surround with deviled eggs and sprigs
of watercress.

Serves 4 to 6

Cucumber Cream Salad

1 small package lime gelatin
1 cup hot water
1 teaspoon salt
2 tablespoons vinegar
1 teaspoon onion juice
1/2 cup mayonnaise
1 cup sour cream
2 cups cucumber,
    finely chopped and drained

Dissolve gelatin in hot water; chill until slightly thickened. Add remaining ingredients, combining well. Pour into mold that has been lightly coated with mayonnaise. Refrigerate until firm. Unmold on bed of greens and garnish with cherry tomatoes.

Aunt Blanche's Ribbon Salad

1 small package gelatin in your
    preference each: green, orange,
    yellow and red colors
4 cups hot water
2 cups cold water
2 cups milk
1 cup sugar
2 envelopes unflavored gelatin
1/2 cup cold water
1 pint sour cream
2 teaspoons vanilla

Dissolve each package of gelatin separately in 1
cup hot water. Add 1/2 cup cold water to each.
Coat a 9x13x2-inch pan with mayonnaise and pour
green gelatin into this pan. Set aside other colors.
Bring to a boil 2 cups milk: add sugar, stirring
until dissolved. In another dish dissolve the unflavored gelatin in 1/2 cup cold water. Add this to
milk and sugar mixture, mixing well. Add sour
cream and vanilla, beating well: cool. Pour 1 1/2
cups of this white mixture on top of jelled green
gelatin. When white mixture is firm, add orange
gelatin. Repeat process for yellow gelatin, ending
with the red gelatin on top.

Cherry Bourbon Salad

3 ounces black cherry gelatin
1 cup boiling water
3/4 cup cherry juice
1/4 cup bourbon
Juice of 1 lemon
16-ounce can black seedless cherries, drained
8 marshmallows, cut into fine pieces
3/4 cup pecans, toasted and chopped

Stir gelatin into hot water until dissolved. Add cherry juice, bourbon and lemon juice. Chill until slightly congealed. Add remaining ingredients and pour into oiled mold. Place in refrigerator until congealed.

Serves 6 to 8

Congealed Lemon and Pimiento Cheese Salad

3-ounce package lemon gelatin
1 cup boiling water
1/2 cup sugar
1 small jar pimiento cheese spread
1 small can crushed pineapple, drained
9-ounce carton whipped topping
1 cup toasted pecans, if desired

Dissolve gelatin in boiling water. Add sugar and cheese spread. Mix well. Add drained pineapple. Let congeal to consistency of unbeaten egg whites. Fold in whipped topping and pecans. Pour into oiled ring mold. Place in refrigerator to congeal.

Serves 6 to 8

Grapefruit Pineapple Salad

3 ounces lemon gelatin
1 cup hot ginger ale
Pinch of salt
1 tablespoon vinegar
1 tablespoon sugar
1 grapefruit, sectioned
1 small can crushed pineapple, undrained
Toasted pecans

Add gelatin to hot ginger ale, stirring until completely dissolved. Chill slightly and add remaining
ingredients. Pour into ring mold that has been
lightly coated with mayonnaise. Place in refrigerator until congealed. Chopped maraschino cherries
may be added for color if desired.

Serves 6

Louise Dunn's Ginger Salad

16-ounce can white
   Queen Anne cherries, chopped
16-ounce can spiced peaches, cubed
Orange juice or cooking sherry
1 small package lemon gelatin
1 small package orange gelatin
1/2 cup chopped pecans
1/2 cup crystallized ginger

Drain fruit, saving juices. Add orange juice or sherry to make 3 cups liquid. Heat to almost boiling and add gelatins, stirring well. Chill until almost syrupy. Add remainder of ingredients. Pour into 2-quart mold. Top with dressing when chilled, if desired.

Dressing
1 egg yolk
1/4 cup honey or maple syrup
3/4 cup cream, whipped
Juice of 1 lemon

Beat egg yolk well in top of double boiler. Add honey and cook for 1 minute or until thick. Cool and fold in cream; add lemon juice.

Nettie's Apricot Congealed Salad

1 small package lemon gelatin
1 large can apricots, drained and blended
Pinch salt
Juice of one lemon
Juice of one orange
8-ounce package cream cheese
3/4 cup toasted nuts, chopped

Dissolve lemon gelatin in one cup boiling apricot juice. Add blended apricots, salt, lemon juice and orange juice. Form cream cheese and nuts into balls and place in center of individual molds that have been coated with mayonnaise. Pour gelatin over cream cheese and nut balls. Refrigerate.

Serves 6 to 8

A recipe from Mrs. East, one of the best cooks I have ever known. Everything she did was wonderful. I called one time and asked if she could bake me some cookies. She asked how many. When I told her 3,500 she screamed and said "not that many!" Several days later she called to tell me my cookies were ready.

Ozie's Congealed Chicken Curry Asparagus

12 to 16 asparagus spears,
 cooked reserving liquid
1 small box lemon gelatin
Sliced stuffed olives
1 2/3 cups chicken stock
2 packages unflavored gelatin
1 can cream of chicken soup
1 cup mayonnaise
2 teaspoons curry powder
1 tablespoon Worcestershire sauce
2 1/2 cups cooked chicken
1 cup chopped celery
1/2 cup almonds

Drain liquid from asparagus and add enough water to make 1 1/2 cups. Beat and add to lemon gelatin. Arrange asparagus spears and olives in 2-quart mold. Pour in 1/2 of gelatin mixture. Let jell. Pour in remaining mixture. Combine chicken stock, unflavored gelatin, chicken soup, mayonnaise, curry powder and Worcestershire sauce and cook for 5 minutes. Add cooked chicken, celery and almonds. Chill and pour over gelatin mixture.

Raspberry Jello Mold

3-ounce package raspberry gelatin
3/4 cup hot water
1/2 cup raspberry juice
2 10-ounce packages frozen raspberries

Topping
1 cup small marshmallows
2 tablespoons cream
1/2 envelope unflavored gelatin
1 cup sour cream

Dissolve gelatin in hot water. Drain juice from raspberries; add 1/2 cup raspberry juice to gelatin while still hot. Add berries and pour into mold that has been coated with mayonnaise. Chill.

For topping: Melt marshmallows with cream over low heat. Add gelatin and mix well. Add sour cream, mix and chill. Spread over gelatin mixture after it has congealed.

Serves 6

Raspberries are one of my favorites. This recipe is a must. I always loved standing in my mother's garden eating raspberries picked fresh from the vines.

Congealed Spinach
with Crab Meat Dressing

3 3-ounce packages lime gelatin
3 cups boiling water
1/2 cup cold water
6 tablespoons vinegar
1 1/2 cups mayonnaise
3 cups cottage cheese
4 tablespoons onion, minced
1 cup celery, diced
3 10-ounce packages chopped, frozen
  spinach, thawed and well drained

Crab Dressing

3 cups mayonnaise
3/4 cup chili sauce
2 tablespoons horseradish
1/2 large onion, chopped
Tabasco sauce, optional
2 cups flaked crab meat

Dissolve gelatin in hot water, add cold water and vinegar. Add all other ingredients and pour into a 9x13-inch dish that has been coated with mayonnaise. Refrigerate until congealed.

For dressing:
Mix together all ingredients except crab meat, then fold in crab meat.

To serve, cut congealed mixture into squares and place on lettuce leaf with crab dressing spooned over it. Garnish with tomato wedges.

Serves 12 to 15

Red Russian Salad

2 envelopes unflavored gelatin
1 cup cold tomato juice
2 cups tomato juice, heated to boiling
1/2 cup red Russian dressing
1 cup finely chopped green pepper
1/2 cup finely chopped celery

In a large bowl, sprinkle unflavored gelatin over cold juice; let stand 1 minute. Add hot juice and stir until gelatin is completely dissolved; stir in red Russian dressing. Chill, stirring occasionally, until mixture is consistency of unbeaten egg whites. Fold in green pepper and celery. Turn into an 11x7-inch baking pan or 5 cup mold or bowl and chill until firm.

Serves 6

California Chicken Salad

1/2 cup butter
2 cups mayonnaise
1/4 cup parsley, minced
1/2 teaspoon curry powder
1/4 teaspoon garlic, minced
Pinch of marjoram
Salt and pepper to taste
4 cups cooked chicken breasts,
    shredded (about 4 small breasts)
2 cups seedless green grapes, sliced
1/2 cup toasted, slivered almonds
Lettuce leaves

Melt butter in saucepan. Cool to room temperature. In a bowl, gently stir the butter into mayonnaise, parsley, curry powder, garlic, marjoram, salt and pepper. In a large bowl, combine chicken, grapes and almonds. Arrange this mixture on lettuce leaves. Spoon dressing on top and sprinkle with paprika.

Serves 4

Little ladies can be rude and shove if we happen to run out of California Chicken Salad at noon!

Carolyn's Chicken Salad

1 small cantaloupe, quartered,
    seeds removed
1 cup cooked chicken, cubed
1/2 cup seedless grapes, halved
1/4 cup slivered almonds, toasted
1/2 cup celery, chopped
1/2 cup sour cream
1/4 cup mayonnaise
1 teaspoon soy sauce
1/4 teaspoon salt
1/2 teaspoon curry powder
1/2 tablespoon candied ginger,
    finely chopped
Parsley for garnish

Carefully remove pulp of cantaloupe and cut the
fruit into cubes. Combine cantaloupe, chicken,
grapes, almonds and celery. Fold together sour
cream, mayonnaise, soy sauce, salt, curry and ginger. Carefully add to chicken and grape mixture,
then spoon into cantaloupe shells. Garnish with
parsley.

Serves 4

Chicken Apricot Salad

1/4 cup mayonnaise
1/4 cup sour cream
1 cup yogurt
1/3 cup milk
2 tablespoons lemon juice
2 teaspoons Dijon mustard
1 teaspoon salt
1 cup dried apricots, diced
3 cups cooked chicken, diced
1 cup celery, chopped
1/3 cup finely chopped scallions
Crisp lettuce leaves

Blend mayonnaise, sour cream, yogurt, milk, lemon juice, mustard and salt in large bowl. Add apricots, chicken, celery and scallions. Toss lightly, combining well; chill. Serve on lettuce leaves. Sprinkle with additional apricots if desired.

Curried Chicken Salad Rounds

3/4 cup cooked chicken, cubed
1/2 cup celery, chopped
1 tablespoon minced onion
1 tablespoon lemon juice
1/2 teaspoon curry
1/3 cup mayonnaise
6 slices bread
Butter or margarine
Pineapple slices
8-ounce package cream cheese
2 or 3 tablespoons syrup
   from pineapple
1/4 cup chopped nuts

Combine chicken, celery, onion, lemon juice, curry
and mayonnaise for salad. Cut bread in rounds the
same size as pineapple. Butter bread. Spread
chicken salad on 6 slices. Place on pineapple rings.
Mix cream cheese and pineapple syrup to make
icing. Decorate with pineapple and nuts.

Serves 6

Party Chicken Salad

6 ounces lemon gelatin
2 cups boiling water
2 cups cream, whipped
8-ounce package cream cheese
1 1/2 cups chopped celery
1 cup stuffed olives, sliced

Topping
3 to 4 cups chicken or turkey, diced
1 pint Hellmann's mayonnaise
1 tablespoon onion, chopped
1 1/2 tablespoons lemon juice

Dissolve lemon gelatin in boiling water. Cool.
When it reaches the consistency of egg whites,
fold in whipped cream and cream cheese which has
been softened with a little milk. Add celery and
olives. Fold together gently and pour into a 9 x
12-inch pan that has been coated with mayonnaise.
Chill. For topping, mix all ingredients together.
Place squares of gelatin mixture on lettuce leaves.
Spoon topping on individual servings. Garnish with
tomato wedges, avocado slices or both.

Serves 12 to 15

Cold Beef Salad with Fresh Spinach Dressing

Julienne strips of leftover roast beef
Celery, sliced
Green onions, both white and green
    parts, sliced
Salt and pepper, to taste

Dressing
Mayonnaise
Fresh spinach leaves

Toss beef, celery, and onions together. Place individual servings loosely on lettuce leaves. Place mayonnaise in blender and add fresh spinach leaves until desired color is obtained. Spoon dressing over cold beef and garnish with tomato wedges.

A delicious way of using leftover roast beef. Amounts are not specified because you simply use what you have on hand.

Cooked Pimiento Cheese

1 small can pimiento, chopped
1 pound Velveeta cheese
1 tablespoon flour
5 tablespoons sugar
1 egg
1 tablespoon mayonnaise
1/4 cup vinegar

Place all ingredients in top of double boiler and cook until smooth. Use an electric mixer if necessary. Refrigerate.

My mother obtained this recipe while working at an ordinance plant in Viola, Kentucky during World War II. Good, inexpensive, and keeps well.

Lecie's Blueberry Delight

12 ounces grape gelatin
4 cups boiling water
2 cups crushed pineapple, undrained
2 cups blueberry pie filling

Topping
16 ounces cream cheese
2 cups sour cream
1 cup sugar
Chopped pecans

Dissolve gelatin in boiling water; cool. Add
pineapple and blueberry pie filling. Pour into
9x12-inch oiled pan and let congeal in refrigerator.

For topping:

Combine cream cheese, sour cream and sugar.
Spread over congealed mixture and sprinkle with
chopped nuts.

Serves 12 to 15

Flavors can be changed by using strawberry pie filling and
gelatin, cherry pie filling and cherry gelatin or peach pie filling
with peach gelatin.

Eggless Mayonnaise

1/4 cup thawed egg substitute
1 cup oil
Salt and pepper to taste
Mustard to taste
Vinegar or lemon juice to taste

Place egg substitute in blender container. Process while adding oil slowly until it thickens. Season to taste.

Mary D's
Hot Sweet Mustard

1 cup dry mustard
1 cup sugar
3 eggs, beaten
1 cup cider vinegar

Mix mustard and sugar. Place into heavy saucepan. Add beaten eggs and vinegar. Cook over medium heat, stirring constantly until thickened. Keeps well store in refrigerator.

Very good served with cold baked ham or cold sliced turkey. Also a must for hamburgers.

Miss Jean's Sweet-Sour Dressing

1 cup granulated sugar
1 cup oil
1/2 cup cider vinegar
1 small onion, quartered
Paprika to desired color
1 tablespoon celery seed
1 teaspoon salt

Place all ingredients in blender; blend until smooth.

Mrs. Alben Barkley's Salad Dressing

1 pint olive oil
2/3 cup powdered sugar
Juice of 1 lemon
Juice of 1 orange
3 tablespoons vinegar
1 teaspoon Worcestershire sauce
2 teaspoons paprika
1 teaspoon salt
1 teaspoon onion juice
1/2 teaspoon red pepper

Mix oil and sugar until well blended. Add
remaining ingredients and shake well; refrigerate.
Shake well before serving.

Sour Cream
Roquefort Cheese Dressing

1/4 cup sour cream
1/4 cup mayonnaise
3 tablespoons crumbled
   Roquefort cheese
1 tablespoon sugar
1 tablespoon grated onion
4 teaspoons vinegar

Combine all ingredients. Keeps well refrigerated.

Serves 1

Dijon Dressing

8 ounces Dijon mustard
16 ounces water
2 teaspoons salt
1 tablespoon sugar
1 tablespoon white pepper
1 tablespoon monosodium glutamate
1 medium onion, chopped
2 fresh garlic cloves
2 tablespoons Worcestershire sauce
1/8 cup white vinegar
1 cup oil

Put all ingredients except oil in blender and mix 2 minutes. Add oil and blend for 2 minutes longer. Keeps up to 6 months when refrigerated.

Variations: Substitute 1 cup sour cream or 4 ounces bleu cheese or Roquefort cheese for Dijon mustard. Blend or mix by hand.

Entrées

Froage-Randall House

Baked Chicken Breast with Spinach

4 packages chopped frozen spinach
3 whole chicken breasts, halved
Flour
Melted butter
Salt, pepper and granulated garlic
2 cartons whipping cream
Parmesan cheese
Paprika

Thaw and drain spinach. Pat spinach into buttered
9 x 13-inch casserole dish. Dip chicken breast into
flour and then butter. Place on top of spinach.
Season well with salt, pepper and garlic. Pour
whipping cream over top; sprinkle generously with
Parmesan cheese and dust with paprika. Bake at
325° for 45 minutes to 1 hour.

Serves 6

Parmesan Baked Chicken

4 1/2 cups fresh bread crumbs
1 1/4 cups grated Parmesan cheese
1 teaspoon salt
1/3 cut chopped parsley
1 1/2 cups butter, melted
3 cloves garlic, crushed
1 tablespoon Dijon mustard
2 teaspoons Worcestershire sauce
Three 2 1/2 to 3 pound fryers, cut up

Mix together bread crumbs, cheese, salt and parsley. Spread in shallow pan. Melt butter, add garlic, mustard and Worcestershire sauce. Stir well. Dip chicken into butter mixture, then roll in crumb mixture. Bake at 325° 1 to 1 1/2 hours. Serve warm or room temperature.

Serves 10 to 12

Honey'd Chicken

1/4 cup butter or margarine
1/4 cup honey
1/4 cup prepared mustard
1 teaspoon salt
1 teaspoon curry powder
3 pound broiler/fryer,
   cut into serving pieces

Melt butter over moderately low heat. Add honey, mustard, salt and curry powder. Roll chicken in mixture and arrange single layer in buttered baking dish. Bake at 325° for one hour or until tender. Baste chicken occasionally.

Serves 4

Lemon Marinated Chicken

2 1/2 pounds chicken
1 clove garlic, pulverized
2 tablespoon catsup
1/2 cup lemon juice
1/3 cup salad oil
1 tablespoon Worcestershire sauce
1/2 teaspoon salt
1/4 teaspoon black pepper
1 bay leaf

Cut chicken into pieces. Shake remainder of ingredients to mix well. Marinate chicken 1 to 3 hours. Bake all one hour at 325° uncovered. Serve chicken and marinade over rice.

Chicken Breast with Raspberry Vinegar Sauce

6 chicken breast halves,
  skinned and boned
1 tablespoon oil
1 tablespoon butter
1/2 cup raspberry vinegar
1 cup chicken broth
3/4 cup whipping cream
1/4 cup toasted, chopped,
  slivered almonds
2 tablespoons finely chopped
  fresh parsley

Pound chicken breasts slightly to make even in thickness. Heat oil and butter in skillet. Add chicken breasts and brown all sides until golden; remove. Drain pan of excess fat, then deglaze with vinegar and chicken broth. Return chicken breasts to pan and simmer, covered, for 20 minutes. Remove chicken and place on serving platter. Keep warm. Reduce pan juices to 1/4 to 1/3 cup. This will probably take quite a while. Then add whipping cream. Reduce pan liquids to 1/2 volume (at least 10 minutes). Pour resulting sauce over chicken breasts. Garnish with almonds and fresh parsley.

Breast of Chicken en Croûte

1 whole boneless breast of chicken
1/4 cup clarified butter
2 sheets phyllo dough
1 egg, beaten
1 3/4 ounces Boursin Cheese Stuffing

Cut chicken breast in half and sear in hot clarified butter. Place one sheet of phyllo dough on parchment paper and lightly brush with clarified butter. Cut dough in half and place equal amounts of cheese stuffing, centered, on each side of dough. Place chicken breast on top of stuffing. Fold each side lengthwise and roll up. Brush with egg wash. Bake at 325° for approximately 30 minutes or until golden brown.

Boursin Cheese Stuffing

3 ounces Boursin Cheese
1 ounce butter
1 1/2 ounces chopped pecans

Mix all together and set aside.

Skillet Chicken Stew

6 slices bacon
2 1/2 to 3 1/2 pounds chicken pieces
1 cup onions, chopped
1 cup celery, chopped
2 cups cabbage, chopped
16-ounce can tomatoes, cut in quarters
1 teaspoon salt
1/8 teaspoon pepper

In large electric skillet, cook bacon on medium heat until crisp, remove bacon and turn heat to high. Add chicken and cook about 10 minutes, browning on all sides. Push chicken to one side of skillet, add onions, celery and cabbage. Stir for 5 minutes more. Remove any excess oil. Add tomatoes, salt and pepper; bring to a boil. Cover and simmer over low heat for about 20 minutes or until fork can be inserted in chicken with ease. Crumble bacon on top. May be served over rice.

Serves 4

Savory Oven Fried Chicken

24 chickens, approximately
   2 1/2 pounds each
6 cups flour
3 tablespoons paprika
3 tablespoons salt
1 tablespoon black pepper
6 cups cornflake crumbs
2 tablespoons parsley flakes
2 tablespoons marjoram leaves,
   crumbled
6 whole eggs
1 quart milk
4 cups shortening, melted

Cut chicken into serving sized pieces. Combine flour with paprika. Salt and black pepper. Coat chicken with flour. Combine cornflake crumbs with parsley and marjoram: set aside. Prepare egg wash by beating eggs in a bowl. Add milk and mix well. Dip floured chicken in egg wash, then in seasoned cornflake crumbs. Place half of the shortening in three 12x20x2 1/2" sheet pans. Arrange chicken on pans skin side down. Drizzle remaining shortening over chicken. Bake in a preheated oven at 350° for 45 minutes, turning once during baking.

Serves 48

Chicken and Vegetable Pasta

8 broiler-fryer chicken thighs
2 tablespoons olive oil
3 tomatoes, chopped in chunks
1 rib celery, chopped in chunks
1 large onion, chopped in chunks
3 yellow squash, cut in chunks
3 zucchini squash, cut in chunks
4 tablespoons lemon juice
1 teaspoon basil leaves
1 teaspoon curry powder
1/8 teaspoon salt
8 ounces angel hair pasta,
    cooked according to directions

In Dutch oven, place oil and heat to medium temperature. Add chicken and brown on all sides. Remove chicken and keep warm. Add tomatoes, celery and onion; cook stirring for about two minutes. Add remaining ingredients and cook about two minutes more. Place chicken on top of veggies; cover, reduce to low and cook. Turn chicken several times to coat with sauce. Cook until fork can be inserted easily into chicken, about 20 minutes.

Serves 4

Good one dish meal!

Buttermilk Chicken with Rosemary

4 pound broiling chicken,
  cut into serving pieces
3/4 cup buttermilk
1/2 cup packaged dry bread crumbs
1 1/2 teaspoon salt
1/4 teaspoon black pepper,
  freshly ground
1 teaspoon rosemary leaves, crushed

Place chicken parts in shallow 2 1/2-quart casserole. Pour buttermilk over chicken. Cover and refrigerate for 2 to 3 hours. Mix bread crumbs, salt, pepper and rosemary. Coat each piece of chicken with crumb mixture. Return chicken to buttermilk in casserole. Bake at 325° for 1 1/4 to 1 1/2 hours.

Serves 4 to 6

Chicken a la Jerusalem

2 pounds of chicken,
  cut in serving pieces
1 cup flour
1/4 pound of butter
Salt, pepper, nutmeg
1/2 pound sliced mushrooms
6 fresh or frozen artichoke hearts,
  cooked
1/2 cup cream sherry
Whipping cream
Minced parsley
Minced chives

Dredge chicken in flour, then brown in butter.
Season with salt, pepper, and nutmeg. Add mushrooms and artichokes. Pour sherry over all. Cover
and simmer for 15 minutes, or until tender and
most of wine has evaporated. Stir in cream to
desired consistency. Top with minced parsley and
chives.

Chicken and Artichoke Casserole

3 pound chicken
3 chicken breast halves
1 cup butter
1/2 cup flour
3 1/2 cups milk
3 ounces Gruyere or Swiss cheese
2 cloves garlic, pressed
1/2 teaspoon red pepper
2 8-ounce cans button mushrooms, drained
2 14-ounce cans artichoke hearts, drained and quartered
Hot buttered noodles

Boil chicken in well seasoned water until tender. Cut meat into large pieces and set aside. Melt butter in skillet and blend in flour: add milk slowly, stirring constantly, until thickened. Cut cheese into small pieces and add to sauce, stirring until melted. Add chicken, seasonings, mushrooms and artichoke hearts. Pour into greased casserole: bake at 325° for 30 minutes. Serve over buttered noodles.

Serves 12

Make in advance and refrigerate. Take out of refrigerator, let come to room temperature. Or, take out and increase baking time to 50 minutes.

Chicken and Potatoes Dijon

1 1/3 pounds (about 4 medium) potatoes
4 green onions, sliced
4 chicken breast halves,
   boned and skinned
Salt and pepper to taste
2 cloves garlic, minced
1 tablespoon Dijon-style mustard
2 teaspoons chopped fresh tarragon or
1/2 to 1 teaspoon dried
1/2 cup dry white wine or chicken broth
1/4 cup light sour cream

Pierce potatoes with tines of fork; microwave on High for 10 minutes. Cool for 2 minutes; cut into 1/2" cubes. Spray 12 inch nonstick skillet with cooking spray; add potatoes and onions. Cook over medium heat for 10 minutes, tossing as they cook, adding more cooking spray as necessary. Push potatoes to side of skillet. Add chicken; cook with potatoes about 15 minutes or until potatoes are tender and chicken juices run clear. Season with salt and pepper. Remove chicken and potatoes to platter and keep warm. Add remaining ingredients, except sour cream, to skillet. Cook until reduced by half. Whisk in sour cream. Pour over chicken and potatoes. Serve immediately.

Serves 4

Chicken Croquettes

2 tablespoons butter
2 tablespoons flour
1 cup milk
2 cups chopped chicken
1/2 teaspoon salt
1/2 teaspoon celery seed
1/2 teaspoon chopped parsley
1/2 teaspoon lemon juice
1 teaspoon chopped onion
Pepper to taste

Melt butter in small saucepan. Stir in flour;
slowly add milk. Cook until thickened. In large
bowl, combine remaining ingredients. Add sauce
and mix until it can be handled easily. Spread on
platter and refrigerate for 1 hour. Shape into croquettes, roll in bread crumbs, dip in beaten egg and
deep fry. May be shaped like miniature chickens,
using almond for beak and cloves for eyes. Serve
on bed of parsley.

Chicken Denise

2 tablespoons butter
3 pound chicken, cut up
Paprika
4 medium onions, sliced 1/8 inch thick
8 ounces fresh mushrooms, sliced
2 cups heavy cream
1/2 teaspoon salt

In a 12-inch skillet, melt butter; add chicken, skin side down and sprinkle with enough paprika to cover well. Fry at moderately high heat until browned and barely cooked through – about 15 minutes. Turn chicken skin side up, again sprinkle with enough paprika to cover well; fry for another 15 minutes. Remove chicken, drain fat and reserve 2 tablespoons.

In reserved fat gently cook the onions until translucent. Layer mushrooms over onions and then add chicken. Pour cream over chicken and baste once. Add salt and additional paprika to make sauce a pale orange. Place a sheet of foil over skillet and simmer, stirring occasionally, until sauce is reduced to desired consistency – about 45 minutes to 1 hour. Serve over cooked noodles.

Serves 4 to 6

Chicken Divan Patsy

2 10-ounce packages frozen broccoli
2 cups cooked chicken,
    sliced or 3 cooked chicken breasts,
    boned and sliced
2 cups condensed cream of chicken soup
1 cup mayonnaise
1 teaspoon lemon juice
1/2 teaspoon curry powder
1/2 cup sharp process cheese, shredded
1/2 cup butter crumbs or almonds

Cook broccoli until tender, drain and arrange on bottom of 11 1/2 x 7 1/2" baking dish. Place chicken on top of broccoli. Combine soup, mayonnaise, lemon juice and curry powder. Pour over chicken. Sprinkle with cheese. Top with bread crumbs or sliced almonds. Bake at 325° for 25 to 30 minutes. Trim with pimento strips if desired.

Serves 6 to 8

Chicken Paprikash

3 pound chicken, cut into serving pieces
Salt and pepper
2 tablespoons butter
1 cup onions, thinly sliced
1 tablespoon garlic, finely minced
1 tablespoon sweet paprika
1/2 cup fresh or canned chicken broth
1 cup sour cream
1 tablespoon flour

Wash, then sprinkle chicken with salt and pepper to taste. Heat butter in a heavy skillet; add chicken pieces, skin side down. Cook over moderately high heat about 5 minutes. Turn the pieces. Continue cooking until brown on second side. Sprinkle the onions and garlic around chicken pieces. Sprinkle with paprika and stir. Add chicken broth, cover and let simmer until chicken is cooked. Remove chicken to a warm serving dish. Blend sour cream with flour and stir into the sauce. Cook, stirring, about 1 minute. Pour sauce over chicken and serve with noodles.

Serves 4

Chicken Philippe

1/2 pound mushrooms, sliced
3 tablespoons butter
1 frying chicken, cut in pieces
1 teaspoon salt
1/2 teaspoon pepper
1/2 cup oil
1 1/4 cup rice, uncooked
1 clove garlic, minced
3 cups chicken broth
1 jar white onions
   (or 1/2 package frozen whole onions)
1/2 cup dry white wine
1/2 cup slivered almonds, toasted

Sauté mushrooms in butter; remove from pan.
Season chicken with salt and pepper and brown on
all sides in oil. Remove chicken and lightly brown
rice and garlic in remaining oil. Stir in 2 cups of
chicken broth and turn into a large casserole dish.
Arrange chicken, mushrooms and onions on rice.
Mix remaining broth with wine and pour over all.
Cover and bake at 325° for 45 minutes. Uncover
and bake for 30 minutes longer. Top with almonds.

Serves 4 to 6

Chicken fit for a King
    ....or Howard, Bruce and Bill

Sherry's Chicken Tetrazzini

6 to 8 large chicken breasts
1 celery stalk
1 bouillon cube
Salt and pepper
1 medium onion, chopped
1 stick butter
3/4 tablespoon flour
1 can cream of mushroom soup
1/2 cup milk
1 can sliced, drained water chestnuts
1 can chopped ripe olives
2 small jars pimentos,
    drained and chopped
1 can mushrooms and liquid
1 pound Velveeta cheese,
    cut into chunks
Salt and pepper to taste
Dash of garlic powder
10-ounce package egg noodles
1 jigger sherry, optional

Boil chicken with celery, salt, pepper and bouillon cube. Bone and cut chicken in bite size pieces. Sauté onion in butter; blend in flour. Stir in mushroom soup; add milk, water chestnuts, olives, pimentos and mushrooms with liquid. Stir in cheese until it melts. Add chicken, salt, pepper and garlic powder. Preheat oven to 325°. Cook noodles according to directions. Drain and add to chicken mixture. Pour into large casserole; pour sherry on top if using. Bake for 20 minutes or until it bubbles.

Grace Church
Chicken Spectacular

10 3/4-ounce can cream of celery soup,
   undiluted
1/2 cup mayonnaise
1/2 teaspoon salt
Pepper to taste
2 cups rice, cooked
8-ounce can sliced water chestnuts,
   drained
2-ounce jar pimiento, chopped
2 tablespoons onion, chopped
8-ounce can sliced mushrooms
10-ounce package frozen green peas,
   cooked
5 cups cooked chicken, cut into chunks
   (approximately 4 pounds breast
   quarters)
2 cups buttered bread crumbs
Paprika

Mix soup, mayonnaise, salt and pepper well. Add
rice, water chestnuts, pimiento, onion and mushrooms. Blend. Carefully fold in peas and chicken.
Spoon into buttered 9 x 13-inch casserole; top with
bread crumbs and sprinkle with paprika. Bake at
350 degrees for 25 minutes.

Serves 12 to 15

Hot Turkey Casserole

1 to 1 1/2 cups cooked turkey, chopped
1/2 cup mayonnaise
1/2 can cream of chicken soup
1/2 can cream of mushroom soup
2 hard boiled eggs, chopped
1/2 cup toasted sliced almonds
1/2 teaspoon minced onion
1 can water chestnuts, drained
1/2 cup bread crumbs

Mix all ingredients except bread crumbs thoroughly. Place in greased casserole and top with crumbs. Bake at 325° for 20 minutes.

Serves 6

Quail or Dove Pie

6 doves or quail, dressed
1/4 green pepper, diced
1 teaspoon Worcestershire sauce
3/4 stick butter
Salt and pepper to taste
Hard boiled eggs
Pastry for top of casserole dish

Place all ingredients in pan except eggs and pastry. Add water to cover and cook until well done. Remove meat from bones. Thicken juice with flour, add meat and place in casserole. Top with sliced hard boiled eggs. Cover with pastry. Brown in 350° oven.

Serves 4

Stuffed Peppers

6 green peppers
3 tablespoons onion, chopped
2 tablespoons butter
1 pound ground chuck
1/2 cup cooked rice
1/2 teaspoon salt
1/4 teaspoon black pepper
2 8-ounce cans tomato sauce
1/2 cup sour cream
1/4 cup sherry
1/2 pound sharp cheddar cheese, grated

Remove stem ends and seeds from peppers. Sauté onion in butter, add meat and brown. Mix in rice, salt, pepper and 1 can tomato sauce. Fill peppers and arrange in baking dish. Combine sour cream, the remaining can of tomato sauce and the sherry; pour over peppers. Bake at 325° for 45 to 60 minutes. Sprinkle with cheese and bake another 15 minutes.

Serves 6

A natural for summer menus when peppers are plentiful.

Roast Tenderloin of Beef

1 beef tenderloin, trimmed
Butter
Salt and pepper to taste
1/3 cup beef consommé
2 tablespoons tomato puree
1/4 cup sherry

Begin with tenderloin at room temperature and rub with butter, salt and pepper. Roast the beef at 325° for 30 to 40 minutes. During roasting time, baste with two tablespoons butter 2 or 3 times.

Remove tenderloin from pan. To the juices add the consommé, tomato puree and sherry. Let boil and pour over tenderloin. Serve thinly sliced, hot or cold.

Serves 6 to 8

Mexican Torte

3 pounds ground beef,
  browned and drained
3 cups chunky style salsa
1/2 cup sliced green olives
1/2 cup sliced green onion
1 package 10-inch flour tortillas
1 cup melted butter or margarine
12 to 15 slices cheddar cheese
12 to 15 slices Monterey Jack cheese
3 or 4 tomatoes, sliced, reserving one
2 cups sour cream

Combine ground beef, salsa, olives and green onion
in a mixing bowl. Set aside. Place first tortilla
on greased baking sheet that has at least 1-inch
sides. Brush butter on tortilla then spread about
1 1/2 cups of the beef mixture on the tortilla.
Spread to edges then top with slices of cheddar and
Monterey Jack cheese, and slices of tomato.
Butter second tortilla on both sides; place on top.
Repeat layering beef mixture, cheeses and tomato
until you have five to six layers. Place last tortilla on top with cheeses only. Bake at 325° for
35 to 40 minutes or until heated through.

If torte begins to brown too much, cover loosely
with foil. Slices of tomato can be placed on top
during the last five minutes. When baked let sit
before slicing and garnish with sour cream.

Little Mushroom Beef Stanley

Eight 6-ounce steak fillets
1/2 stick butter
1 small onion, chopped
4 green onions with tops, chopped
3 ribs celery, chopped
1/2 pound mushrooms, sliced
1 small green pepper, chopped
15-ounce can tomato puree
1 tablespoon seasoned salt
Pepper to taste
4 large bananas,
    sliced lengthwise then crosswise, once
Cinnamon and sugar

Sauce
1 cup sour cream
1 1/2 teaspoons horseradish
1/2 teaspoon Worcestershire sauce

Season steaks with salt and pepper and broil on
low heat for about 10 minutes. In a saucepan,
sauté onions, celery, mushrooms and green pepper
in butter until soft. Add the tomato puree, seasoned salt and pepper and pour over the steaks.
Bake at 325° for about 25 minutes. Top each

steak with two slices of banana which have been sprinkled with cinnamon and sugar and bake at 325° until soft. Combine the sour cream, horse-radish and Worcestershire sauce and let stand at room temperature. Spoon over steaks.

Serves 8

Spiced Salt

3/4 cup salt
2 tablespoons sugar
2 tablespoons paprika
2 teaspoons ground black pepper
2 teaspoons onion powder
2 teaspoons hot dry mustard
2 teaspoons ground allspice
1 teaspoon garlic powder
2 teaspoons ground coriander

Mix all ingredients well and store in tightly cov-ered containers or salt or seasoning shakers

Use as an all-purpose seasoned salt for eggs, pota-toes or salads.

Makes 1 1/4 cups

Loaf Made with Leftover Meats

3 cups ground cooked meat
    (ham, pork, veal or beef)
1 small onion
Parsley
2 eggs, beaten
1/4 teaspoon pepper
1/2 cup sifted bread crumbs
1 tablespoon prepared mustard
1 cup tomato juice

Grind meat with onion and parsley. Add remaining ingredients. Pack into well greased loaf pan and bake 40 minutes in 325° oven.

Serves 6

John Marzetti

1 pound ground beef
Salt and pepper
1 large onion, chopped
10-ounce can tomatoes
10-ounce can tomato juice
1 small can mushrooms
1 package noodles
1/2 package Velveeta cheese
1 green pepper

Sear meat; add salt, pepper and chopped onion. After this is well seared add tomatoes and tomato juice. Cook until they are boiling rapidly. Dice mushrooms and add to mixture; let cook for ten minutes. Cook noodles in salted water; add to mixture and cook for 15 minutes. Add cheese and cook until melted; add green pepper. Serve immediately.

Easy dish to do if pressed for time. Serve with green salad and a crusty bread.

Curtis' German-Style Roast

3 pound chuck roast
Three 27-ounce cans sauerkraut,
 drained
One 1-pound box light brown sugar
One 28-ounce can chopped tomatoes
 and juice
2 medium onions,
 peeled and thinly sliced
2 Granny Smith apples, cored,
 peeled and thinly sliced
Fresh ground pepper

Put roast in heavy saucepan or Dutch oven.
Layer sauerkraut, brown sugar, tomatoes, onion
and apples. Cover and simmer on low for 4 hours
or until meat falls apart. Can be cooked in 275
degree oven for 4 to 5 hours. Can be chilled
overnight and served after removing fat. Freezes
well and keeps for one week.

Serves 6 to 8

Breaded Veal in Milk

Veal round steaks, cut into servings
Salt and pepper to taste
1 egg, beaten
Cracker crumbs
Milk

Sprinkle veal steaks with salt and pepper. Dip in beaten egg, then in cracker crumbs. Fry in hot fat until golden brown. Cover with milk; let cook slowly for about one hour.

Veal Vermouth

1 1/2 pounds thin veal steaks
2 tablespoons flour
1/4 cup butter
1 clove garlic, minced
1/2 pound mushrooms, sliced
1/2 teaspoon salt
Dash of pepper
1 tablespoon lemon juice
1/3 cup dry vermouth
2 tablespoons parsley, snipped

Flatten veal to 1/4 inch thick. Cut into 1-inch squares and flour. Melt butter and sauté veal, a little at a time, until golden brown on both sides. Return all meat and the garlic to the skillet and heap mushrooms on top. Sprinkle with salt, pepper and lemon juice. Pour on vermouth, cover and cook over low heat for 20 minutes or until veal is fork tender. Add a little more vermouth if needed. Sprinkle with parsley just before serving.

Serves 4

This dish can be prepared ahead and reheated in the oven.

Sweet and Sour Pork

2 pounds lean pork,
  cut into 1/2 inch cubes
1/4 cup vegetable oil
1 cup chicken stock
2 green peppers, cut into eighths
1 cup pineapple chunks, drained
3 tablespoons flour
2 tablespoons soy sauce
1/2 cup vinegar
1/2 cup sugar
1/2 teaspoon salt
1/4 teaspoon black pepper

Brown pork in vegetable oil. Do not let pieces of
pork touch when browning. Remove pork from
skillet as it browns. Drain skillet, place pork back
into skillet. Add stock, green peppers, pineapple
chunks, flour which has been mixed with soy sauce
and vinegar, sugar, salt and pepper. Simmer 15
minutes.

Serve hot over cooked rice.

Serves 6

Sausage Rice Casserole
by Maxine Hearell

2 pounds pork sausage
1 cup bell pepper, finely chopped
1 cup onion, chopped
2 1/2 cups celery, coarsely chopped
2 small packages instant
    chicken noodle soup
4 1/2 cups boiling water
1 cup rice, uncooked
1/2 teaspoon salt
1 cup blanched almonds, optional
1/4 cup butter, melted

Brown sausage, pour off excess fat. Add bell pepper, onion and one cup of celery to sausage and sauté. In a large pan add soup mix to boiling water, stir in rice, cover and simmer for 20 minutes or until tender. Add sausage mixture and salt, stirring well. Pour into buttered baking dish and sprinkle remaining celery and almonds over the top. Drizzle with melted butter. Bake uncovered at 325 degrees for about 30 minutes.

Serves 12 to 14

Portuguese Pork Tenderloin

2 pounds pork tenderloin
2 tablespoons flour
Salt, pepper and paprika
3 tablespoons butter
1 onion, sliced
1/2 pound mushrooms, sliced
2/3 cup dry white wine
1/8 teaspoon rosemary
2 tablespoons lemon juice
2 tablespoons parsley, chopped

Season flour with salt, pepper and paprika. Roll tenderloin in seasoned flour. Sauté pork in butter until golden brown. Add sliced onions and mushrooms; sauté for a minute or two. Add wine and rosemary. Cover and cook over low heat for 45 to 60 minutes, or until tenderloin is done. Add lemon juice and parsley just before serving.

Serves 4 to 6

Pineapple Spareribs

3 pounds meaty spareribs
Salt and pepper to taste
1/2 cup onion, finely chopped
1/4 cup green pepper, chopped
1/4 cup brown sugar
1/2 teaspoon dry mustard
16 ounces tomato sauce
1 tablespoon Worcestershire sauce
1/3 cup vinegar
20-ounce can pineapple tidbits
    with juice

After every third rib, cut about halfway through
the strip. Sprinkle with salt and pepper. Place in
shallow roasting pan. Bake at 325° for 1 to 1 1/4
hours. Carefully pour off all excess fat. While
ribs are roasting, mix remaining ingredients and let
stand to blend flavors. Pour over ribs after 1 to 1
1/4 hours of baking. Bake 45 to 50 minutes,
basting frequently to glaze the ribs with the fla-
vorful sauce.

Serves 4

Blue Cheese Stuffed Pork Chops

1 stick butter
1 large onion, chopped
1 cup mushrooms, sliced
1/4 pound blue cheese, crumbled
Croutons or dry bread crumbs
Salt and pepper to taste
6 one-inch pork chops cut with pocket

Melt butter, sauté onion and mushrooms in butter.
Remove from heat. Stir in crumbled blue cheese.
Add enough croutons or bread crumbs to absorb
moisture. Mix well and stuff into chops. Bake,
uncovered, at 350 degrees for one hour or until
done. Baste with drippings occasionally while
cooking.

Serves 6

People in western Kentucky or the entire state never tire of
country ham. We can travel 60 miles north into Southern
Illinois and the guests like it but they don't fall onto the floor
and kick. I had bought a very good ham in the country, with
white streaks and prepared it for a party in the north. I served
it sliced on a silver tray and beautifully garnished. A man
came up to me and said, "That is the best corned-beef I ever
put into my mouth." I could not tell him the difference.

Pork & Cornbread Pie

2 tablespoons oil
1 medium onion, diced
2 minced garlic cloves
2 pounds pork, cut in 1-inch chunks
28 ounces tomatoes
4 ounces chopped green chilies, drained
2 teaspoons brown sugar
Salt to taste
1/2 cup plain flour
1/2 cup plain cornmeal
2 tablespoons sugar
1 1/2 teaspoons baking powder
1/3 cup milk
1 large egg

Sauté onion and garlic in oil until tender, stirring
occasionally. Transfer to a small bowl. Cook pork
chunks in remaining oil over medium heat until well
done. Brown on all sides; return onion mixture to
skillet. Stir in undrained tomatoes, green chilies,
brown sugar, 3/4 teaspoon salt and 1/2 cup water.
Bring to boil over high heat, stirring to loosen
brown bits from bottom of skillet. Spoon mixture
into deep 2 1/2-quart casserole. Cover and bake
at 325° for 1 hour. Five minutes before pork is
done, prepare cornbread topping. Into a medium
bowl, mix flour, cornmeal, sugar, baking powder.

and 1/4 teaspoon salt. With fork, stir in milk, egg and tablespoons salad oil just until blended. Remove casserole from oven. Skim off fat from liquid in casserole. Gently spread batter over top of casserole. Bake 20 minutes, or until toothpick comes out clean and meat is fork tender.

Pork Tenderloin

8 to 10 bacon strips
4 pork tenderloins
1/2 cup soy sauce
1 tablespoon onion, grated
1 clove garlic, minced
1 tablespoon vinegar
1/4 teaspoon black pepper,
   freshly ground
1/4 teaspoon seasoned salt
1/2 cup granulated sugar

Wrap bacon around tenderloins and secure with tooth picks; place in baking dish. Combine remaining ingredients and pour over tenderloins. Place in refrigerator and let stand 4 to 5 hours, turning often. Bake at 300° for 1 1/2 to 2 hours, basting often. Turn meat once. Serve juice separately.

Serves 10 to 12

Orange Ginger Pork Chops

Six 1-inch pork chops
1/4 cup orange juice
1/2 teaspoon salt
1 teaspoon ground ginger
6 orange slices (one large orange)
3 tablespoons cornstarch
3/4 cup dairy sour cream

In a skillet coated with cooking spray, brown chops well over medium heat, about 10 minutes per side. Add orange juice, cover and simmer about 30 minutes. Uncover, sprinkle chops with salt and ginger and top each with orange slice. Cover and cook 10 to 15 minutes more or until chops are fork tender. Transfer chops to an ovenproof platter and top each with sour cream. Place under broiler about one minute. Serve immediately.

Serves 6

Country Barbecued Spareribs

2 ounces salt
16 racks of spareribs

Country Barbecue Sauce 1 gallon

2 quarts tomato catsup
1 quart chili sauce
1 pint water
1 1/2 cups vinegar
1 cup onion, minced
1/2 cup brown sugar, firmly packed
2 tablespoons salt
2 tablespoons dry mustard
2 tablespoons paprika
4 teaspoons garlic salt
1 tablespoon celery salt
2 teaspoons chili powder
2 teaspoons black pepper

Combine all sauce ingredients in a large saucepan. Bring to the boiling point. Reduce heat and simmer for 20 minutes, stirring occasionally.
Salt ribs. Arrange in shallow roasting pan meat side up. Bake in preheated oven at 375° for 30 minutes, turning once. Drain fat. Brush on Country Barbecue Sauce generously. Reduce temperature to 325° and continue baking 45 minutes longer, basting ribs every 15 minutes with remaining sauce.

Serves 48

Charlie's Sausage Casserole

1 pound flat Italian macaroni
3 pounds bulk pork sausage,
 cut into bite size pieces
2 to 3 green peppers, sliced
1 large onion, sliced
2 4-ounce cans tomato paste
1 29-ounce can tomatoes
2 tablespoons butter
1 pound of fresh mushrooms,
 halved or quartered
Salt and cracked pepper to taste
Grated Parmesan cheese

Cook the macaroni in boiling water until done.
Rinse in cold water and drain. Brown the sausage
in frying pan; remove with slotted spoon. Brown
green pepper and onion in drippings; add tomato
paste and tomatoes. In another skillet, sauté the
mushrooms in butter until they are light brown.
Combine the macaroni, meat, vegetables and seasonings. Place in large shallow casserole and
refrigerate overnight. Bake at 325° for 1 1/2
hours. Sprinkle Parmesan cheese generously over
top and reheat for a minute or two.

Serves 16 to 18

Chas and Jo Moore always served for brunch.

Filet of Sole Veronique

1 pound sole or flounder fillets
Salt
1 tablespoon lime juice
1 teaspoon dried parsley
1/4 teaspoon tarragon
1/2 clove garlic, minced
3/4 cup white wine
1/4 pound seedless green grapes
1 1/2 tablespoons butter
1 tablespoon flour
2 tablespoons orange juice

Sprinkle fish fillets lightly with salt and lime juice. Place in lightly greased skillet. Sprinkle with parsley, tarragon and garlic. Add wine and simmer 12 to 15 minutes until fish flakes easily with fork and looks milky white, not transparent. Add grapes the last five minutes. Remove fish and grapes and keep warm on separate platter.

In the original skillet, melt butter with remaining juices and blend in flour until smooth. Add orange juice and cook, stirring until mixture thickens. Add more wine if desired. To serve, pour sauce over fillets.

Serves 3 to 4

Norma's Salmon Patties

15-ounce can salmon
1 tablespoon prepared mustard
1 egg
2 tablespoons vinegar
1/2 cup onion, chopped medium fine
2 tablespoons flour
Salt and pepper to taste
1 cup cracker crumbs,
    about 24 to 26 soda crackers

Mix all ingredients except cracker crumbs. Break up salmon and mash any soft bone pieces; mix well. Heat shortening or 1/4-inch of cooking oil in skillet on medium heat. Dip about 1/2 cup salmon mixture in cracker crumbs, working in a small amount of crumbs. Coat with crumbs again and shape into patties about 1/2-inch thick. Gently place in heated oil. Cook until golden brown on both sides. Oil should be hot enough to start browning, so as not to soak up oil. Remove from skillet and drain on paper towels.

Shrimp Newburg

4 tablespoons butter
4 tablespoons flour
1/2 teaspoon salt
Black pepper, freshly ground
2 cups milk
2 egg yolks, slightly beaten
1 1/2 pounds shrimp, cooked and peeled
1/4 cup sherry

Melt butter over low heat. Add flour, salt and pepper slowly, stirring constantly, until smooth. Add the milk slowly, stirring constantly, until thickened. Add a little of the hot milk mixture to the slightly beaten egg yolks, then return them to the milk. Stir and cook for about 2 additional minutes. Add shrimp and heat thoroughly (do not boil). Add sherry; stir well and serve on toast points or in individual ramekins.

Serves 4

Delicate, rich and creamy.

Joyce's Rock Shrimp with Tomatoes & Feta Cheese

1/4 cup olive oil
1/2 cup chopped onion
2 cloves garlic, minced
4 medium tomatoes, peeled, seeded
    and chopped; or 2 16-ounce cans
    whole peeled tomatoes,
    drained and chopped
1/2 cup dry white or red wine
1/4 teaspoon sugar
1 1/2 teaspoons each fresh
    minced oregano, basil and thyme
    or 1/2 teaspoon each dried
2 tablespoons parsley
1 1/2 pounds medium rock shrimp,
    shelled and deveined
1/4 pound Feta cheese,
    cut in 1/4" cubes
12 Greek or Italian Olives
Salt and pepper to taste

Sauté onions and garlic in oil. Add tomatoes, wine, sugar, spices and 1 tablespoon parsley. Cook 3 to 5 minutes over medium high heat until reduced slightly. Reduce heat to medium, add rinsed and dried shrimp. Cook just until shrimp are firm and pink. Gently add cheese and olives; salt and pepper to taste. Sprinkle with rest of parsley.

Serves 4 to 6

Shrimp Creole

2/3 cup onion, chopped
1/2 cup green pepper, chopped
1/2 cup celery, chopped
2 tablespoons butter
16-ounce can tomatoes
8-ounce can tomato sauce
2 cloves garlic, minced
2 bay leaves
1 teaspoon salt
1/4 teaspoon pepper
1/2 teaspoon oregano
Celery salt to taste
1 1/2 pounds shrimp, cooked,
    peeled and deveined

Sauté onions, green pepper and celery in butter.
Add tomatoes, tomato sauce and seasonings.
Simmer for about 40 minutes. Add cooked shrimp
just before serving. Serve over cooked rice.

Serves 4 to 6

A recipe from Marie Knight's mother.

Creole is from New Orleans, where seafood is an everyday
ingredient in their cuisine. This dish is so quick and easy, you
will want to serve it frequently.

Crab Quiche

13 ounces crab meat
4 eggs
2 cups half and half
1 1/2 teaspoons salt
2 teaspoons dry Vermouth
2 teaspoons grated onion
6 ounces Gruyere cheese, grated
8 ounces Swiss cheese, grated
2 teaspoons flour
2 pinches nutmeg
1/4 teaspoons pepper
2 unbaked pie shells

Preheat oven to 325°. Bake pie shells for 5 to 10 minutes. Beat eggs, cream and remaining ingredients. Mix well and pour into pie shells. Bake for 30 to 35 minutes.

Fish Pudding From Calvary Church

3 pounds red snapper
   or other favorite fish
3 eggs, beaten
1 cup milk
1 stick butter, melted
1 cup cracker crumbs
1 tablespoon parsley, chopped
1 tablespoon onion, grated
Juice of one lemon
Salt and pepper to taste
Sherry to taste

Bake fish with a little seasoning. Bone and flake. Place in a bowl and add eggs, mixing well. Add milk and one half butter, one half of the cracker crumbs, parsley, onion, lemon juice, salt, pepper and sherry. Mix, then place in buttered baking dish. Top with remaining cracker crumbs and butter. If mixture appears to be dry, add a little more milk. Place baking dish in pan of hot water and bake at 325° for about 50 minutes. Serve with tartar sauce.

Serves 8 to 10

Seafood Casserole

1 stick butter
1 cup celery, chopped
1 cup green pepper, chopped
1 pound mushrooms, chopped
1 cup onions, chopped
2 pounds shrimp, cooked
1 can crab meat
1/2 pound sharp cheese, grated
1/2 cup wild rice, cooked
1/2 cup white rice, cooked
4 tablespoons butter
4 tablespoons flour
2 cups meat
Salt and pepper

Melt butter and sauté celery, green pepper, mushrooms and onions. Add shrimp, crab meat, cheese and rice. Make cream sauce of butter, flour and milk. Add ingredients to cream sauce. Correct seasonings. Place in buttered casserole. Bake 45 minutes at 325 degrees.

Serves 10 to 12

Springtime Spaghettini

2 tablespoons salt
1 pound very thin egg noodles
1/4 cup butter
2 teaspoons minced garlic
2 large carrots, cut julienne
1 medium zucchini, cut julienne
1 small red or green pepper, cut julienne
1 cup whipping cream
1/2 cup freshly grated Parmesan cheese
1/4 cup chopped fresh dill
    or 1 1/3 tablespoons dried dillweed
1/2 teaspoon salt
1/4 teaspoon freshly ground pepper

Cook noodles in water with 2 tablespoons salt to
al dente. Meanwhile, melt butter in large pan
over medium high heat. Add garlic and sauté about
1 minute. Add vegetables and toss over high heat
for 2 minutes. Drain pasta. Place vegetables
over high heat. Stir in cream, 1/2 cup Parmesan,
dill, salt and pepper. Add pasta to skillet and toss
gently to blend. Divide among 6 heated plates.
Garnish with dill. Pass additional Parmesan
cheese.

Serves 6

James Beard's Pasta with Primavera Sauce

1 cup small broccoli florets
1 small zucchini, sliced
1 small sweet red pepper, cut into strips
1/2 cup Chinese snow peas, optional
1/4 cup butter or margarine, unsalted
1 cup half and half or cream, warmed
Freshly ground black pepper to taste
1 pound spaghetti or other pasta,
   cooked and drained
Grated Parmesan cheese

In large skillet sauté broccoli, zucchini, red pepper and snow peas in butter until crisp-tender. Add half and half and black pepper; cook briefly until slightly reduced. Serve over pasta and sprinkle with Parmesan.

Serves 4

*T*ry using any combination of vegetables that are available.

*S*ince primavera means early spring, a primavera sauce should be made with the first tiny spring vegetables. In the winter use the freshest vegetables available.

Norma's Eggplant with Cheese & Tomatoes

1 medium eggplant, pared and
    cut in 1/2" thick slices
1/2 cup olive or salad oil
1/4 cup tomato sauce or barbecue sauce
1/4 cup grated Parmesan cheese
1 teaspoon salt
1 teaspoon oregano
3 large tomatoes, peeled and
    cut in 1/2" slices
3 slices mozzarella cheese

Brown eggplant slices in oil and drain. Mix
together tomato sauce, Parmesan cheese, salt,
oregano and pepper. In a casserole, make 2 layers
each of eggplant and tomato slices with sauce mixture divided between each layer. Bake, uncovered,
in preheated 325° oven for 30 minutes. Arrange
mozzarella on top and bake 15 minutes longer.

Sometimes I add sliced onion and mushrooms.

Vegetables & Sides

Purcell - Fitzpatrick House

Irene's Baked Acorn Squash with Orange Sauce

4 medium Acorn Squash

Orange Sauce
1 cup water
2 cups orange juice
1/2 teaspoon orange rind, grated
2 cups sugar
1/4 cup butter
3/4 teaspoon salt
1/4 teaspoon nutmeg

Cut squash in half lengthwise. Remove seeds and membrane. Place cut side down in a baking dish and bake at 300° for 45 minutes. Turn cut side up and spoon sauce over each piece. Continue baking until squash is tender. Brown under broiler if desired.

Orange Sauce:
Simmer all ingredients in heavy saucepan over low heat about thirty minutes or until syrupy.

Serves 8

Shredded Beets with Tarragon

5 medium size raw beets
1/4 to 1/3 cup butter
2 to 3 tablespoons tarragon vinegar
1 teaspoon fresh tarragon
   (or 1/2 teaspoon dried)
1 small clove garlic, peeled
Salt and pepper to taste
1 teaspoon sugar

Wash and scrub beets but do not peel. Shred raw beets, using coarse grater or processor. Melt butter; add vinegar and tarragon. Stick a toothpick in garlic clove and drop in pan. Add shredded raw beets, a dash of salt and pepper and stir to combine. Cover pan and simmer 8 to 15 minutes, just until tender and crisp. Stir several times during cooking to combine ingredients. Instead you may microwave on high power for 5 to 6 minutes. Remove from heat, take out garlic clove, add sugar and stir. Taste again and adjust seasonings.

Serves 4 to 6

Broccoli

2 packages frozen broccoli
1 cup mayonnaise
1 cup cream, whipped
1 teaspoon salt
2 eggs, beaten

Cook broccoli in lightly salted water until tender crisp; drain. Combine remaining ingredients and cover broccoli with sauce. Bake at 325° for 25 minutes. This can be done in advance. Keep refrigerated and bake an extra 10 minutes.

Serves 4 to 6

Toot Smith's Broccoli Mold

2 packages chopped frozen broccoli
1 1/2 envelopes unflavored gelatin
1 cup beef bouillon
3-ounce package cream cheese, softened
1 hard boiled egg, grated
1/2 to 3/4 cup mayonnaise
Dash Tabasco sauce
1 tablespoon Worcestershire Sauce
1 tablespoon onion, grated
Salt and pepper to taste

Cook broccoli according to directions. Drain well. Sprinkle gelatin over beef bouillon and heat to dissolve. Add cream cheese to bouillon mixture, stirring to blend. Add broccoli, grated eggs, mayonnaise, Tabasco, Worcestershire, onion and seasonings. Place in mold that has been coated with mayonnaise. Chill until firm. Good served as salad or cold vegetable.

Serves 6 to 8

Carrots, Artichoke Hearts and Mushrooms

2 cups fresh mushrooms, sliced
2 tablespoons butter
1 tablespoon salad oil
2 tablespoons green onions, chopped
1 pound carrots, quartered and cooked
10-ounce package
   frozen artichoke hearts, quartered
1/2 cup beef broth
Salt and pepper to taste
Chopped parsley

Sauté mushrooms in butter and oil. Add onions and cook until tender. Add carrots, artichokes, beef broth, salt and pepper. Cover and simmer about 5 minutes. Sprinkle with chopped parsley.

Serves 8

Marinated Carrots

2 pounds carrots
1 onion
1 cup chopped green pepper
3/4 cup sugar
1/2 cup oil
1/2 cup vinegar
1 small can tomato sauce
1 small can Snappy Tom

Slice carrots lengthwise and cook to just tender.
Slice onion and break into rings. Add to carrots
during the last 5 minutes of cooking time. Drain
carrots and add green peppers. Combine sugar, oil,
vinegar, tomato sauce and Snappy Tom. Pour over
carrot mixture and marinate 3 days. Will keep in
refrigerator for 2 weeks.

Serves 12

Carrot Ring

2 cups carrots, shredded and cooked
1 1/2 cups American cheese, grated
2 eggs, separated and beaten
1 cup milk
1 cup coarse cracker crumbs
Salt and pepper

Combine drained carrots, cheese, egg yolks, milk, cracker crumbs, salt and pepper. Fold in beaten egg whites. Place in well greased ring mold. Place mold in a pan of hot water and bake at 325° for one hour or until firm.

Serves 6 to 8

Corn Pudding

2 cups milk
1/4 cup bacon drippings
4 slices bread
4 eggs, beaten until fluffy
2 10-ounce packages frozen whole
    kernel corn or creamed
1/2 bell pepper, diced
1/2 cup sugar
Salt and pepper to taste
1 cup cheddar cheese, grated

Combine milk and bacon drippings. Pour over bread slices and soak. Break slices into pieces then mix in eggs. Add mixture to corn seasoned with bell pepper, sugar, salt and pepper. Bake at 325° for 30 minutes or until slightly browned. Top with grated cheese just as you take it from the oven.

Serves 8 to 10

Baked Eggplant

1 medium eggplant
Salt water
1 can tomato soup
1 finely chopped onion
1 finely chopped green pepper
Celery seed
Dash curry powder
1 tablespoon butter
Salt
Red pepper
2 eggs, hard boiled and chopped
Cracker crumbs
Cream

Peel eggplant, then cut into pieces and boil in salt water until tender. Mash fine. Cook tomato soup, onion, green pepper, celery seed, curry powder, butter, salt and red pepper in skillet. When thick, add eggplant and hard boiled eggs. Pour into buttered baking dish. Top with cracker crumbs and a little cream. Bake at 325° until hot and bubbly and crumbs are browned.

Serves 6

Janet's Eggplant Casserole

Sliced eggplant, unpeeled
Sliced onions,
   uniform in size to eggplant
Mozzarella cheese, grated
Can of tomato sauce

Layer bottom of ovenproof casserole with
ingredients in order listed. Bake at 325° for 15 to
20 minutes, or as Janet says "until you are ready
to eat – 1 Scotch – 2 Scotches, whatever it takes!"

Oven Fried Eggplant

1 medium eggplant
1/4 cup mayonnaise
1/4 cup grated Parmesan cheese
1/2 cup soda crackers, crushed fine

Slice eggplant into 1/2-inch thick slices, but do not peel. Spread mayonnaise in thin layer on both sides of eggplant slices. Mix cheese and cracker crumbs and coat eggplant. Place slices in single layer on baking sheet which has been sprayed with cooking spray.

Bake at 425°. After 10 minutes, turn and continue baking for 5 minutes or until browned and tender. Serve with Yogurt Dressing or lemon wedges.

Yogurt Dressing

1 cup unflavored yogurt
1/2 cup sour cream
1/2 teaspoon onion powder
Juice of 1/2 lemon (about 1 tablespoon)
Dash garlic powder

Combine all ingredients and mix well.

Serves 6

Lima Beans Spanish Style

1 1/2 cups cooked lima beans
2 cups tomatoes
1 teaspoon salt
2 tablespoons chopped onion
1 tablespoon butter, melted
1/2 cup cracker crumbs
3 slices bacon

Mix first four ingredients. Pour into a buttered baking dish. Mix butter and crumbs and sprinkle on top. Arrange bacon strips on top and bake at 325° for 25 minutes.

Lima Bean Casserole

2 packages frozen lima beans
Butter, salt and pepper to taste
1 medium size can pimento, chopped
8 ounces sour cream
2 tablespoons milk or cream
Parmesan cheese

Cook lima beans in small amount of water; drain and season with butter, salt and pepper. Add remaining ingredients and pour into buttered casserole. Sprinkle generously with Parmesan cheese. Bake at 325° for 30 to 40 minutes.

Serves 6 to 8

Upon arriving at a private home to serve a very special dinner party, I discovered that I had left behind the handle to my silver chafing dish. I couldn't drive 40 miles back home to get it. So, I broke the handle off a wooden spoon, found the black shoe polish and applied it to the wood, and stuck it into the dish. No one ever noticed the difference.

Stewed Green Beans with Tomato and Mint

2 cups finely chopped onion
1/3 cup olive oil
4 large garlic cloves, minced
2 tablespoons dried mint, crumbled
1 28-ounce can plum tomatoes,
    drained and chopped
Juice from tomatoes
Salt and pepper to taste
2 pounds green beans, trimmed

In skillet, cook onion in oil over moderately low heat, stirring occasionally until softened; add garlic and mint. Cook mixture, stirring constantly, for 2 minutes. Add tomatoes and tomato juice, salt and pepper to taste. Simmer for 15 minutes, stirring occasionally. Add beans and simmer, covered, stirring occasionally, for 30 minutes or until beans are very tender.

Beans improve in flavor if made at least 1 day and up to 3 days in advance, cooled to room temperature, and kept covered and chilled. Serve beans at room temperature or heated.

Serves 6 to 8

Miriam's Marinated Vegetables

1 large can sliced mushrooms
1 can water chestnuts, sliced
1 small can pitted ripe olives, sliced
1 small can stuffed olives, sliced
1 large can artichoke hearts, cut up
1 large can Italian green beans
4 green onions, sliced
Seasoned salt
1/2 cup cider vinegar
1/3 cup oil
2 tablespoons dill weed
1/2 cup sugar

Drain all vegetables. Make 3 layers in any order. Sprinkle each layer with seasoned salt. Combine vinegar, oil, dill weed and sugar. Pour over vegetables and marinate in refrigerator for 24 hours.

Serves 10 to 12

Mushroom Strudel

1 pound mushrooms, minced
1/2 cup minced yellow onions
1 cup minced green onions
1 tablespoon oil
1 1/2 sticks butter, divided
1/4 teaspoon Tabasco
1/2 cup sour cream
2 tablespoons minced fresh dill
   or 1 tablespoon dried basil
1/2 teaspoon salt
1/2 teaspoon pepper
6 to 8 phyllo leaves, moistened,
   placed under a damp tea towel

Preheat oven to 350°. Placed mushrooms, a hand-ful at a time, in a tea towel and squeeze out all the moisture. In a skillet, sauté mushrooms and onions in oil and 3 tablespoons butter until mois-ture has evaporated, about 15 minutes. Remove from heat and stir in Tabasco, sour cream, dill, salt and pepper. Let mixture cool thoroughly.

Melt remaining butter. Place one phyllo leaf on a sheet of waxed paper and brush gently with melted butter. Spread a 1-inch wide strip of mushroom mixture along one of the long sides of the leaves, fold in the sides of the leaves to contain the filling,

and roll up the leaves jelly-roll fashion. Transfer the roll to a buttered baking sheet, with seam side down. Repeat procedure for remaining phyllo leaves: brush with melted butter and bake at 325° for 45 minutes until crisp and golden. Allow the rolls to cool 5 minutes. Cut rolls on an angle in 1-inch slices. Serve warm.

Makes 4 dozen

Popcorn Balls

5 quarts popped corn
2 cups sugar
1 1/2 cups water
1/2 teaspoon salt
1/2 cup light corn syrup
1 teaspoon vinegar
1 teaspoon vanilla
Candy red hots

Keep popped corn hot in slow oven 300°. Butter sides of saucepan. Combine next 5 ingredients in pan: cook to hard ball stage (250°). Mix in vanilla. Add to popped corn along with candy red hots. Butter hands lightly: form into 2 1/2" small balls.

Makes 30

Jane's Potatoes Nicoise

1 clove garlic
3 medium potatoes (1 pound)
3 large medium-ripe tomatoes
Boiling water
3 red onions
1/4 teaspoon dried tarragon leaves
1/4 teaspoon dried basil leaves
1 1/2 tablespoons parsley, chopped
2 teaspoons salt
1/4 teaspoon nutmeg
2 tablespoons butter
1/2 cup cheddar or Gruyère cheese,
   grated

Rub baking dish with garlic. Pare potatoes and slice 1/4-inch thick. Scald tomatoes in boiling water. Peel and slice 1/2-inch thick. Slice onions thin. Layer potatoes, onions and tomatoes in baking dish with tomatoes last. Combine herbs and seasonings. Sprinkle over top. Dot with butter. Cover and bake at 400° for 45 minutes. Uncover. Sprinkle with cheese and bake 15 minutes longer.

Potato Cakes Southwestern Style

6 cups shredded potatoes
1 1/2 cups shredded zucchini
1/2 cup chopped green onion
2 tablespoons butter
2 tablespoons salad oil
1/2 cup sour cream
1/2 cup salsa

In bowl combine potatoes, zucchini and green onion. In 10" nonstick skillet heat butter and oil over medium heat. Add potato mixture and cook 15 minutes. Place cookie sheet over skillet and invert. Slide mixture back into skillet; cook 15 minutes longer. Slide onto serving plate. Top with sour cream and salsa.

Serves 6

*H*earty recipe good for Sunday Brunch with fried or barbecued chicken.

Sweet Potatoes

6 medium sweet potatoes
3/4 cups granulated sugar
1 tablespoon cornstarch
1/2 teaspoon salt
1 tablespoon orange rind, grated
1 cup orange juice
2 tablespoons butter

Peel and slice sweet potatoes. Place potatoes in casserole. Put remaining ingredients in heavy saucepan. Cook over medium heat, stirring until slightly thick. Pour over potatoes and bake, covered, at 325° for one hour.

Serves 8 to 10

Raisins may be added if desired.

Sweet Potato Casserole

3 cups cooked sweet potatoes, mashed
1/2 stick butter, melted
1 cup sugar
1 cup coconut
1 teaspoon vanilla
Dash of salt

Topping
1/2 cup flour
1 cup light brown sugar
2/3 stick butter
1 cup pecan pieces

Add melted butter to potatoes. Stir in remaining potato ingredients and pour into greased baking dish. For topping mix flour and sugar. Cut in butter until crumbly. Add nuts and sprinkle mixture on top of potatoes. Bake at 325° for 30 to 45 minutes.

Serves 8 to 10

Baby Vidalia Onion Pie

2 pounds baby Vidalia onions,
    thinly sliced
1 stick butter
3 eggs, well-beaten
1 cup sour cream
1/4 teaspoon salt
1/2 teaspoon white pepper
1/4 teaspoon Tabasco sauce
1 pastry shell, unbaked
Grated Parmesan cheese

Sauté onions in butter. Combine eggs, sour cream, seasonings and Tabasco sauce. Add to onion mixture and pour into pastry shell. Top with cheese. Bake at 450° for 20 minutes, reduce temperature to 325° and bake an additional 20 minutes.

*Lots of possibilities for luncheon dishes by adding cooked diced ham, tuna or chicken. Use your imagination.

Tomato Pudding

18-ounce can tomato puree
1/4 cup boiling water
1 cup brown sugar
1/4 teaspoon salt
1 cup fresh white bread cut in 1" squares
1/2 cup melted butter

Mix puree, sugar and salt together. Boil 5 minutes. Place bread squares in casserole, pour melted butter over. Add hot tomato mixture. Bake, covered for 30 minutes in 325° oven.

Baked Stuffed Tomatoes

8 medium sized tomatoes
1 1/4 teaspoons salt, divided
2 cups zucchini, finely chopped
2 small onions, chopped
1/4 cup green pepper, finely chopped
1/2 teaspoon minced garlic
1/2 teaspoon sugar
3 tablespoons olive oil, divided
1/2 cup soft breadcrumbs
1/4 cup chopped parsley, divided
1 tablespoon dried basil
2 teaspoons red wine vinegar
3/4 teaspoon ground pepper
Collard green leaves
Endive

Cut top quarter off tomatoes. Chop top quarter
and set aside. Scoop out pulp; sprinkle inside of
tomatoes with 1/8 teaspoon salt and invert on
paper towels to drain. Combine zucchini, onion,
green pepper, garlic, sugar, reserved tomato and 2
tablespoons olive oil in a large skillet. Cook until
vegetables are tender. Remove from skillet with
slotted spoon. Add remaining 1 tablespoon olive oil
to skillet; add breadcrumbs and cook until golden.
Add to vegetable mixture. Stir in parsley, basil,

vinegar, pepper and remaining 1/4 teaspoon salt.
Spoon mixture into tomato shells and place in
lightly greased 9x13" baking dish. Sprinkle with
remaining parsley and bake at 325° for 10 minutes.
Garnish serving platter with collard leaves and
endive.

Serves 8

Vegetable Pie

1 pound fresh mushrooms, sliced
1 onion, sliced
2 zucchini or yellow squash, sliced
1 green pepper, sliced
3 or 4 tablespoons butter
1 teaspoon salt
1/4 teaspoon black pepper
Dash garlic salt
10-inch pie shell, baked at
    325 degrees for 20 minutes
1 tomato, sliced
1 cup mayonnaise
1 cup Mozzarella cheese, grated

Sauté vegetables in butter until crisp, but not soft. Drain well and add seasonings. Place tomato slices in bottom of pie shell. Add vegetables. Spread mayonnaise-cheese mixture over vegetables. Bake uncovered at 325 degrees for 45 minutes to 1 hour.

Serves 6

Swissed Vegetables on Toast

2 16-ounce cans mixed vegetables
1/4 cup flour
3-ounce package cream cheese, cubed
1/4 cup milk
1/4 teaspoon onion powder
2 cups fully cooked ham, cubed
1/2 cup processed Swiss cheese, shredded
Toast points

In 10-inch skillet, stir undrained mixed vegetables into flour. Add cream cheese, milk and onion powder; cook and stir over medium heat until mixture is thickened and bubbly. Stir in ham and Swiss cheese; cook until cheese melts. Serve over toast points.

Serves 6

Yellow and Green Squash Sauté

2 medium zucchini
2 medium yellow squash
1/2 cup pitted black olives
2 tablespoons unsalted butter
1 teaspoon oregano
2 dashes hot pepper sauce
1/4 teaspoon salt
1/4 teaspoon black pepper,
   freshly ground

Remove stem and bud ends from zucchini and squash. Slice both into 1/4-inch thick rounds. Slice olives into 1/4-inch rounds. In a large nonstick skillet, heat butter over medium heat. Add zucchini and squash, stirring to coat with butter. Sauté until crisp-tender, about 5 to 7 minutes. Stir in olives, oregano, hot pepper sauce, salt and pepper. Stir to mix seasonings.

Serves 4

Skillet Summer Squash

1/2 cup onion, chopped
1/2 cup green pepper, chopped
2 tablespoons butter
1 tablespoon sugar
1 teaspoon flour
Salt and pepper to taste
2 cups pattypan squash, cubed
3 medium tomatoes, peeled and diced

Sauté onion and green pepper in butter until tender. Stir in sugar, flour, salt and pepper. Add squash and tomatoes; cook over low heat until vegetables are tender.

Serves 4

So many good and interesting things can be done with our regional foods. Why not take advantage of them?

Squash Casserole

2 pounds yellow squash, cut into chunks
1 medium onion, chopped
1 cup cheddar cheese, grated
1 tablespoon sugar
2 eggs, beaten
3 tablespoons butter, melted
1 teaspoon sage
Salt and pepper to taste
Paprika

Cook squash in small amount of boiling water just until tender; drain. Combine all of ingredients except for half of cheese and paprika. Place into buttered casserole; sprinkle with remaining cheese and paprika. Bake at 325° for about 25 minutes or until mixture bubbles.

Serves 6 to 8

Zucchini Casserole

2 zucchini, sliced 1/2-inch thick
6 tablespoons butter
3/4 cup carrots, shredded
1/2 cup onions, chopped
2 1/2 cups herb stuffing mix
1 can cream of chicken soup
1/2 cup sour cream

Boil or steam zucchini until almost tender; drain well. Heat four tablespoons butter in a large skillet; sauté carrots and onions in butter until soft. Add 1 1/2 cups stuffing mix, soup, and sour cream. Add zucchini and toss lightly. Put in a 1 1/2-quart casserole. Melt remaining butter and toss with rest of stuffing mix. Sprinkle this mixture over top of casserole and bake at 325° for 30 to 40 minutes.

Serves 6 to 8

Zucchini Tomato Pie

2 cups chopped zucchini
1 cup chopped tomato
1/2 cup chopped onion
1/3 cup grated Parmesan cheese
1 1/2 cups milk
3/4 cup biscuit mix
3 eggs
1/2 teaspoon salt
1/4 teaspoon pepper

Mix all ingredients and pour into a greased pie plate. Bake at 325 degrees for 30 to 40 minutes.

Serves 6

Lenora Marshall's Wild Rice Casserole

1 1/2 cups wild rice, uncooked
4 cups boiling water
6 tablespoons cooking oil
1 pound ground beef
6 tablespoons onion, chopped
2 cans chicken and rice soup
2 teaspoons salt
1/4 teaspoon each: onion salt,
    celery salt and garlic salt
16-ounce can mushrooms
1 teaspoon soy sauce
Pinch of paprika
Trace of curry
1 bay leaf
1 pound cheddar cheese, grated

Pour boiling water over rice and let stand 15 minutes. Drain. Sauté ground beef and chopped onion in oil. Drain. Combine rice, ground beef and remaining ingredients except cheese. Place in covered casserole dish and bake at 350 degrees for 30 minutes. Remove from oven and sprinkle with cheese. Bake 30 minutes more.

Serves 6 to 8

Very good served with crusty French bread, butter and a tossed salad.

Julie's Rice Pilaf

4 tablespoons butter
1 onion, finely chopped
1 1/2 cups long grained rice
3 cups chicken stock
Salt and pepper to taste

Melt butter in heavy sauce pan and sauté chopped onion in butter. Add rice and cook one minute. Pour on chicken stock, add salt and pepper and bring to a boil. Reduce heat, put on heavy lid and simmer until all liquid is absorbed, about 23 minutes. Remove lid and fluff rice with two forks.

Serves 6 to 8

To Freeze Stock

Freeze meat or chicken stock in ice cube trays. Put in plastic bags and keep in freezer to season sauces and soups. Remove frozen cubes as needed.

Bulgar Pilaf

3/4 cup finely chopped onion
2 tablespoons unsalted butter
1 cup bulgar (cracked wheat)
1 teaspoon freshly grated orange rind
1/4 cup raisins
1 3/4 cups canned chicken broth
Salt and pepper
6 tablespoons pine nuts, toasted lightly
1/4 cup minced fresh parsley leaves
1/4 cup thinly sliced scallion greens

In saucepan, cook onion in butter, stirring until softened. Stir in bulgar and orange rind. Cook mixture for 1 minute. Add raisins, broth, salt and pepper to taste. Bring to boil and cook, covered, over low heat for 10 to 15 minutes, or until liquid is absorbed. Fluff with fork and let cook for 15 minutes. May be prepared up to this point 6 hours in advance and kept chilled, covered loosely, until 30 minutes before serving. Fluff pilaf with fork and stir in pine nuts, parsley and scallion greens.

Serves 5 to 6

Cracked Wheat Pilaf

1 cup cracked wheat
1/4 cup finely chopped onion
1 tablespoon oil
2 cups chicken broth

Sauté wheat and onions in oil to toast wheat, but not brown onion. Add broth and bring to boil; stir, reduce heat, cover and simmer until all liquid is absorbed, about 20 to 30 minutes. Fluff with fork and leave uncovered to dry slightly before serving. Pilaf should not be stirred with a wooden spoon as this mushes cereal.

Serves 4 to 6

Cranberry Casserole

3 cups apples, chopped and unpeeled
2 cups raw cranberries
1 1/4 cups sugar
1 1/2 cups quick-cooking oats, uncooked
1/2 cup brown sugar, packed
1/3 cup flour
1/3 cup pecans, chopped
1/2 cup butter, melted

In 2-quart casserole, combine apples, cranberries and sugar; top with mixture of remaining ingredients. Bake at 325° for one hour or until bubbly and lightly browned. Serve hot.

Serves 8

*G*ood with chicken or turkey.

Hot Fruit Casserole

28-ounce can peach halves
28-ounce can peach slices
15 1/4-ounce can pineapple chunks
17-ounce can apricot halves
17-ounce jar Kodota figs
16-ounce can pitted dark cherries
2 cans slivered toasted almonds
3 to 4 bananas
Lemon Juice
Brown Sugar
Butter
6 dozen almond macaroons

Drain fruit. Crumble macaroons but leave in small pieces as you do not want crumbs. Slice bananas and sprinkle with lemon juice. Mix all fruits together. Layer half fruit and half macaroons in 2-quart casserole. Sprinkle liberally with brown sugar and almonds and dot with butter. Repeat. Bake at 300° for 20 to 30 minutes or until hot and bubbly.

Serves 20 people and will fill 2 casserole dishes

Desserts

Wisdom-Flood House

Aunt Ruth's Dried Apple Cake

2 1/2 cups dried apples, cooked
1 cup butter, room temperature
2 cups sugar
4 cups flour
4 teaspoons soda
4 teaspoons cinnamon
4 teaspoons nutmeg
1 box raisins, dusted with flour
1 cup dates, chopped
1 cup pecans, chopped

Mix apples, while still hot, with butter and sugar.
Add remaining ingredients. Bake at 300° for 1
1/2 hours in a greased and floured tube pan.
Remove from oven, let cool for 10 minutes.
Remove from pan and cool completely. Wrap with
cloth soaked in wine. Store in airtight container.

A wonderfully heavy moist cake.

Bourbon Cake

1 package Duncan Hines
   yellow cake mix
1 package instant vanilla pudding mix
4 eggs
1/2 cup Wesson oil
1/2 cup water
1/2 cup bourbon
1 cup nuts, chopped

Sauce
1/2 cup bourbon
1/2 cup butter
1/2 cup sugar

For cake: Mix all ingredients for one minute.
Pour into greased tube pan and bake at 325° for
50 to 55 minutes.

Sauce: Boil ingredients in heavy saucepan until
dissolved. Pour over cake while still warm.

Serves 12 to 16

Note: You may make a rum cake by using rum instead
of bourbon.

Cherry Chocolate Cake

1 package butter chocolate cake mix
3 eggs
21-ounce can cherry pie filling
1 cup sugar
5 tablespoons butter
1/3 cup milk
1 6-ounce package semi-sweet
   chocolate chips

Mix first 3 ingredients until well blended. Pour
into a greased and floured 9 x 12- inch pan and
bake at 325° for 35 to 40 minutes. For icing,
combine sugar, butter, and milk. Bring to a boil,
stirring constantly; boil for 1 minute. Remove
from heat and stir in chocolate chips, blending until
smooth. Spread on cake.

Chocolate Chip Cake
from Hannah Till

1 box yellow cake mix
1 small box instant vanilla pudding
1 small box instant chocolate pudding
4 eggs
1 1/2 cups water
1/2 cup oil
1 6-ounce package chocolate chips

Empty cake mix and puddings into bowl. Stir until
mixed, then add eggs, water and oil. Blend well,
then beat for 2 minutes at medium speed. Add
chocolate chips and stir in with a spoon. Bake in a
greased and floured bundt pan at 325° for 1 hour.
Cool for 20 minutes and remove from pan. Ice
with your favorite icing or sprinkle with powdered
sugar.

So good it makes you want to slap your grandmother.

Cocoa Roll and Frosting

5 eggs, separated
1 cup sugar
1/4 cup cocoa
1/4 cup flour
1 teaspoon vanilla
1 cup whipped cream

Chocolate Fudge Frosting
1/2 stick butter or margarine
2 squares bitter or
   semi-sweet chocolate
1 cup granulated sugar
1 small can condensed milk
1 teaspoon vanilla

Preheat oven to 350°. Beat yolks slightly, add sugar. Beat until light and thick. Add cocoa, flour and vanilla. Fold in stiff whites. Grease a 10 x 16-inch shallow pan. Line with waxed paper and grease again. Spread batter in pan. Bake 10 to 15 minutes. Turn out on damp towel dusted with confectioner's sugar. Pull off paper quickly and roll while hot. When cold, unroll and spread with sweetened whipped cream and roll again. Cover with chocolate fudge frosting.

For frosting: melt butter and chocolate in double boiler. Add sugar and condensed milk. Remove from heat when thick; add vanilla. Ice top and sides of roll with one-half of frosting. When serving, heat remainder of chocolate and serve as a sauce to be poured over cake slices.

Macaroon Sponge Cake

1 cup sifted sugar
3 eggs, beaten separately
1 teaspoon lemon juice
1 cup sifted flour
1 rounded teaspoon baking powder
1 tablespoon water

Icing
1 dozen macaroons
1/2 cup butter
1 cup powdered sugar
2 egg yolks
Almond extract
1/2 pint whipped cream

Cream sugar and yolks, add lemon juice. Sift flour
and baking powder; add water and flour
alternately. Fold in well-beaten egg whites.
Bake in 9 x 13-inch pan about 30 to 40 minutes.
Cut cake in half.

For icing: Finely crush macaroons, reserving 1/2
cup for sides and top of cake. Cream butter, sugar,
yolks and almond extract. Add whipped cream and
mix in crushed macaroons.
Frost cake, covering top and sides with reserved
macaroon crumbs.

Serves 12 to 15

Crumb Cake

2 cups biscuit mix
1/2 teaspoon cinnamon
1/2 cup sugar
1/4 cup butter or margarine, softened
2 eggs plus enough milk to make 1 cup
1 teaspoon vanilla extract

Topping
1/3 cup packed brown sugar
3 tablespoons butter or margarine

Preheat oven to 325°. Grease and flour a 9"
layer cake pan. Mix topping ingredients until
crumbly. Beat everything together except topping
mix. Pour into pan and sprinkle with topping; bake
20 minutes or until cake tests done.

Snow Ball Cake

2 packages unflavored gelatin
4 teaspoons cold water
1 cup boiling water
1 cup crushed pineapple, undrained
1 cup sugar
1/2 teaspoon salt
1/2 teaspoon lemon juice
3 envelopes Dream Whip
   (prepared according to
   package directions)
1 angel food cake
Coconut

Dissolve gelatin in cold water; add boiling water
and set aside to cool. Combine pineapple, sugar,
salt and lemon juice; add to gelatin mixture. Let
this congeal slightly and fold in two envelopes of
prepared Dream Whip. Remove brown crust from
angel food cake and break into bite size pieces. Line
bowl with wax paper or foil. Alternate layers of
gelatin mixture with layers of cake pieces. End
with a layer of congealed gelatin mixture. Let
stand overnight in refrigerator.

Turn out onto cake plate. Top with remaining
envelope of prepared Dream Whip and cover with
coconut. Store in refrigerator.

Snowy White Frosting

4 egg whites
2 tablespoons water
1/4 teaspoon cream of tartar
1/2 teaspoon salt
4 1/2 cups powdered sugar
2 teaspoons vanilla
Maraschino cherries

Combine egg whites, water, cream of tartar and salt in large bowl. Beat at high speed of electric mixer until egg whites are stiff but not dry. Gradually add powdered sugar and beat until stiff peaks form. Fold in vanilla. Frost cake layers. Top with maraschino cherries.

Sausage Cake

1 pound bulk pork sausage
2 cups brown sugar
1 cup granulated sugar
3 cups flour
1/2 teaspoon baking powder
1 teaspoon soda
1 teaspoon cloves
1 teaspoon allspice
1/2 teaspoon ginger
1 teaspoon cinnamon
1 cup coffee
1 cup nuts
1 cup dates, chopped

Cream sausage and sugars. Sift dry ingredients together. Introduce dry ingredients and coffee alternately to creamed sausage and sugar mixture. Fold in nuts and dates that have been dusted with flour. Bake at 325 degrees in greased and floured tube or loaf pan for 1 hour to 1 hour, 15 minutes.

Serves 16 to 18

Sunshine Cake

1 1/2 cups granulated sugar
1/2 cup water
6 eggs, separated
1 teaspoon orange,
    vanilla or lemon extract
1 1/4 cups cake flour
1/2 teaspoon cream of tartar
1/2 teaspoon salt

Orange Butter Icing
1 cup powdered sugar
Orange juice
Soft butter
1 tablespoon grated orange rind

Cook sugar and water until it spins a thread
(230°). Beat egg whites until stiff but not too
dry. Pour on syrup and continue beating until
cool. Add beaten egg yolks and extract. Sift
flour, cream of tartar and salt several times.
Fold in quickly. Pour into an ungreased angel cake
pan. Bake at 325° for one hour. Cool for one
hour. Spread with Orange Butter Icing.

For Orange Butter Icing: sift powdered sugar
and add orange juice, butter and rind until mixture
is thin enough to spread.

Toasted Spice Cake

3/4 cup shortening
2 cups sifted brown sugar
2 eggs, separated
1 teaspoon soda
1 1/4 cups sour milk
2 1/2 cups flour
1 teaspoon baking powder
1 teaspoon cloves
1 teaspoon cinnamon
3/4 teaspoon salt
1 teaspoon vanilla

Brown Sugar Meringue
2 egg whites
1 cup sifted light brown sugar
1/4 cup broken nuts

Blend shortening, sugar and eggs together. Dissolve soda in sour milk. Add alternately with all sifted dry ingredients. Add vanilla. Mix to smooth mixture. Pour into greased 8 x 12-inch pan. Spread batter with Brown Sugar Meringue. Bake at 350° for 45 to 50 minutes.

Angel Food Chocolate Torte

1 large angel food cake
1 cup sweet butter
2 1/2 cups confectioner's sugar, divided
1 1/2 teaspoons vanilla, divided
2 ounces unsweetened chocolate, melted
6 tablespoons cocoa
1/8 teaspoon salt
2 cups heavy cream
1/2 cup salted pistachio nuts, optional

Slice cake into three layers. Beat 2 cups confectioner's sugar into butter and cream well. Add 1 teaspoon vanilla and melted chocolate. Mix well and spread between layers. Mix and sift 1/2 cup confectioner's sugar, cocoa and salt. Add to cream and chill 2 hours. Add 1/2 teaspoon vanilla to cream and whip until stiff. Spread on top and sides of cake. Chill thoroughly.

Serves 12 to 16

Janice Grace's Schaum Torte

6 egg whites
2 cups sugar
1 teaspoon vanilla
1 teaspoon vinegar
Strawberries
Whipped cream

Whip egg whites until stiff. Gradually add sugar, then vanilla and vinegar. Pour into greased springform pan and bake at 300° for 1 hour.

Serve topped with strawberries and whipped cream.

Betty's Chocolate Pie

1 1/4 cups sugar
3 tablespoons flour
2 tablespoons cocoa
1 small can Pet milk
1 1/2 cups sweet milk
3 egg yolks, beaten
1 1/2 tablespoons butter
1 teaspoon vanilla
Pinch of salt
1 graham cracker crust

In heavy saucepan mix sugar, flour and cocoa.
Add Pet milk and sweet milk. Cook over medium
heat, stirring constantly until thickened. Add a
portion of hot custard to egg yolks; then add yolks
to custard mixture. Remove from heat and add
remaining ingredients. Pour into graham cracker
crust and top with meringue or cool completely and
garnish with whipped cream just before serving.

Serves 6

Betty Lawson would serve this when she had us to dinner.
She used a graham cracker crust, sometimes sweetened whipped
cream on top and at other times a baked meringue. Both are
delicious.

Hershey Bar Pie

6 small Hershey bars with almonds
17 marshmallows, quartered
1/2 cup milk
1 cup cream, whipped
Graham cracker crust

Melt Hershey bars, marshmallows and milk in top
of double boiler. Let cool, then add whipped cream.
Pour into a 9-inch graham cracker crust and place
in refrigerator. Serve with a small amount of
shaved or slivered bitter chocolate on top of each
piece.

Serves 6

Bunny's Devastating Chocolate Fudge Pie

1/2 cup butter
3 1-ounce squares
    unsweetened chocolate
4 eggs, beaten
3 tablespoons light corn syrup
1 1/2 cups granulated sugar
1/4 teaspoon salt
1 teaspoon vanilla
1 9-inch pastry shell, unbaked

In top of double boiler, over boiling water, heat butter and chocolate, stirring until melted, and blended; allow to cool slightly. Blend syrup, sugar, salt and vanilla into beaten eggs. Add chocolate mixture; blend well. Pour mixture into pie shell. Bake at 325° for 45 minutes or until pie is almost but not quite firm when shaken.

Serves 6 to 8

Black Bottom Pie

2 cups ginger snap crumbs
5 tablespoons butter
2 cups milk
4 egg yolks
1/2 cup sugar
1 1/2 tablespoons flour
1 envelope unflavored gelatin
1/4 cup cold water
1 1/2 squares unsweetened chocolate
1 teaspoon vanilla
1 teaspoon rum or whiskey
4 egg whites
1/2 teaspoon baking powder
1/2 cup sugar
1/2 cup whipped cream

Combine ginger snap crumbs with butter; press into
a 12-inch pie plate. Bake 10 minutes in a slow
oven. Let cool.

Cook milk, egg yolks, sugar and flour into a boiled
custard. Soak gelatin in cold water. Reserve 1 cup
of custard.

Melt chocolate and add to custard. Add vanilla
and beat with electric mixer. Pour into cooled

crust and chill. Add soaked gelatin to reserved custard. Stir until dissolved. Cool, but do not let stiffen. Add rum or whiskey.

Beat egg whites, baking powder and sugar into a stiff meringue. Add to gelatin mixture and pour over chocolate mixture. Chill. Top with whipped cream, if desired, and shake a small amount of chocolate on top.

Bourbon Chiffon Pie

1 1/2 cup graham cracker crumbs
6 tablespoons sugar
6 tablespoons melted butter
1/2 teaspoon nutmeg
1 envelope unflavored gelatin
1/2 cup cold black coffee
2/3 cup sugar, divided
1/2 teaspoon salt
3 eggs, separated
6 tablespoons bourbon
4 tablespoons Kahlúa
1 cup heavy cream, whipped

Combine first four ingredients; press into a 9-inch pie pan; bake lightly at 350°; cool.

Dissolve gelatin in coffee; add 1/3 cup sugar and salt and bring to a simmer. Temper egg yolks with hot mixture and add together. Add bourbon and Kahlúa; chill mixture until it begins to thicken.

Make a meringue with egg whites and remaining sugar; fold the meringue and whipped cream into the mixture; turn into pie shell and chill overnight. Serve with whipped cream flavored with sugar and bourbon. Garnish with shaved chocolate on top.

Served at The Jefferson Street Boarding House in St. Louis.

Coconut Crunch Pie

4 egg whites
Pinch of salt
1 cup sugar
1 teaspoon vanilla
1 cup graham cracker crumbs
1/2 cup coconut
1/2 cup pecans

Beat egg whites at high speed of electric mixer until stiff. Add salt, gradually add sugar and fold in vanilla. Stir in graham cracker crumbs, coconut and pecans. Pour into a well buttered pie pan and bake at 350° for 20 minutes.

Serve with whipped cream or sliced bananas and whipped cream.

Easy Winter Apricot Pie

2 cups dried apricots
1 cup orange juice
Pastry for two pie crusts,
   your favorite recipe
1 tablespoon cornstarch
1/2 cup light brown sugar,
   firmly packed
1/4 teaspoon salt
1 tablespoon butter

Soak apricots in orange juice for 2 hours. While apricots are soaking, prepare your recipe for pie crusts. Line an 8 inch pie dish with crust and let chill.

After 2 hours, drain apricots, reserving 2/3 cup of liquid. Heat cornstarch, brown sugar and salt in saucepan. Gradually stir in the reserved orange juice. Cook mixture over moderate heat until slightly thickened, stirring constantly.

Spread apricots around crust, pour the syrup over and dot with butter. Cover with lattice pastry top or plain slit top and bake at 400° for 12 minutes. Reduce heat to 325° and bake for 20 minutes or until pastry is golden brown.

French Raisin Pie

1 1/2 cups granualted sugar
1 stick butter, melted
1 teaspoon vanilla
3 eggs, beaten
1/4 teaspoon each: all-spice
    and cinnamon
Pinch of salt
1/2 cup raisins
1/2 cup nuts, chopped
9-inch pie shell, unbaked

Combine all ingredients; pour into unbaked pastry.
Bake at 325 degrees for 45 minutes to one hour.

Serves 6

Kresge's Pecan Pie

3/4 cup sugar
1 heaping tablespoon flour
3 eggs, beaten
1/2 cup heavy cream
1 cup white syrup
1/2 stick butter, melted
1/2 cup pecans, chopped
1 teaspoon vanilla
Unbaked 9-inch pastry shell

Mix flour and sugar; add to beaten eggs, cream and white syrup. Mix in pecans, melted butter and vanilla. Pour into unbaked pastry shell. Bake at 350° for 45 minutes to one hour.

Serves 6

*U*nder the management of Mrs. Nance and pastry cook, Mrs. Moore, it was well worth waiting in line at Kresges for their delicious foods and desserts: fresh strawberry pie, pecan pie, cobblers, tulip sundae, watching their fresh cake donuts being made and don't forget those foot-long hot dogs!

Peach Crumble Pie

9-inch pastry shell, 2 inches deep,
   unbaked
6 cups fresh peaches, sliced
1 1/2 cups sugar
3 tablespoons cornstarch
Pinch of salt
1 egg, beaten
1/2 teaspoon almond flavoring
1/2 cup flour
1/4 cup butter

Place peaches in pastry shell. Blend 1 cup sugar,
cornstarch and salt: add egg and flavoring. Pour
mixture over peaches. Combine flour and remaining
sugar: cut in butter until fine crumbs are formed.
Sprinkle crumb mixture over peaches. Bake at
325 degrees about 45 minutes or until golden
brown.

Serves 6 to 8

Good to add fresh blueberries over peaches.

Sour Cream and Raisin Pie

4 egg yolks
2 cups sour cream
2 cups sugar
4 teaspoons flour
2 cups raisins
4 egg whites
8 teaspoons sugar, for meringue
One 9-inch baked pastry shell

Put yolks in saucepan and add sour cream, sugar, flour and raisins. Mix well and cook until thick. Pour into pie shell. Beat egg whites with mixer and add 8 teaspoons sugar to form meringue. Spread meringue on top of pie and bake at 400° until brown.

Rhubarb Pie

1 pound frozen or fresh rhubarb
1/2 cup butter, melted
1 1/2 cups sugar
3 tablespoons flour
1/2 teaspoon nutmeg
Pastry for two 9-inch pie crusts

Thaw frozen rhubarb and mix with butter, sugar, flour and nutmeg.

Place into unbaked pie shell, then top with remaining pastry. Brush with butter and sprinkle with sugar. Bake at 350° for 45 minutes to 1 hour or until brown.

Serves 6

Strawberry Pie

1 cup 7-up
1 cup sugar
3 tablespoons cornstarch
3 ounces wild strawberry gelatin
Fresh strawberries, washed and dried

Mix 7-up, sugar and cornstarch. Cook, stirring until thick. Add gelatin. Let cool and add berries. Pour into baked crust and chill. Serve with whipped cream.

Serves 6 to 8

Kathryn's Cheese Cake

2 8-ounce packages cream cheese,
   softened
3 unbeaten eggs
1/2 cup sugar
1/2 teaspoon vanilla
2 cups well drained crushed pineapple
2 1/2 cups graham cracker crumbs
1/2 cup melted butter
2 cups sour cream
3 tablespoon sugar
1 teaspoon vanilla

Mix cream cheese, eggs, sugar, vanilla and pineapple. Beat until well blended. Mix graham cracker crumbs and melted butter together. Reserve 1/3 cup. Pat remainder into a buttered 9-inch spring form pan. Pour in filling and bake ar 325 degrees for 30 minutes. Remove from oven. Mix sour cream, sugar and vanilla together. Cover over filling and sprinkle with reserved crumb mixture. Return to 325 degree oven 5 to 7 minutes. Cool then chill before serving.

This has been presented to us for years by Kathryn. Better every year!

Patsy's Sableé

Sugar Crust:
2 cups flour, sifted
1/2 cup sugar, sifted
1/4 teaspoon baking powder
2 sticks butter, chilled
1 egg yolk
1/2 teaspoon vanilla

Place dry ingredients in bowl and cut chilled butter into flour mixture until size of oatmeal flakes. Add egg yolk and vanilla. Knead with hands until smooth. Place dough in quiche pan and pat to fit. Prick well with fork and bake at 325° for 15 to 20 minutes.

Patsy's Mock Cream Patisserie

2 packages French vanilla instant
    pudding mix
3 cups half and half cream
1/2 teaspoon almond extract
Sliced fruit in season for garnishing

Mix first three ingredients together and allow to
set partially. Pour into sugar crust. Decorate
with fruit and glaze.

Glaze
1/2 cup red currant jelly
1 tablespoon Kirsch or water

Heat jelly until melted. Add the Kirsch or water
and glaze the Sableé.

Caramel Layer Brownies

14 to 16-ounce bag wrapped caramel
   candy chews, unwrapped
   (50 chews)
2/3 cup evaporated milk or
   half and half, divided
1 package German chocolate cake mix
2/3 cup butter, melted
1 cup walnuts or pecans, chopped
12 ounces chocolate chips

Melt together caramels and 1/3 cup evaporated
milk or half and half in top of double boiler; set
aside. Combine cake mix, butter, remaining milk
and nuts. Lightly pat half of mixture in 9 x 13-
inch pan coated with cooking spray. Bake at 350
degrees for 6 minutes. Remove from oven and
sprinkle chocolate chips evenly over cake. Pour
melted caramel over top. Crumble other half of
cake mix evenly over all. Bake 16 to 18 minutes.
Cool and refrigerate a few hours before serving.
Cut into bars.

Chocolate Chip Meringues

2 egg whites
Dash salt
1/4 teaspoon cream of tartar
3/4 cup sugar
6-ounce package chocolate chips
Peppermint to taste

Beat egg whites with salt and cream of tartar until frothy. Gradually add sugar and continue to beat for 15 minutes. Fold in chocolate chips and peppermint. Drop by teaspoonfuls on an ungreased cookie sheet. Place in a preheated 350° oven and turn off oven. Leave in oven for 1 1/2 hours. Do not open oven door to peek.

Makes 36 candies

Chocolate Mint Supremes

1 cup sugar
1 stick margarine, softened
16-ounce can chocolate syrup
1 cup flour
4 eggs, beaten
3-ounce package cream cheese
1/2 stick margarine, softened
4 cups powdered sugar
4 tablespoons milk
3 teaspoons peppermint extract
Green food coloring
6-ounce package chocolate chips
1 stick margarine

Blend sugar, margarine, chocolate syrup, flour and eggs. Pour mixture into a greased 9x13-inch pan. Bake at 350° for 25 minutes. Cool. Beat cheese, softened margarine, powdered sugar, milk and peppermint extract until smooth and creamy. Add a few drops of green coloring. Spread over cooled chocolate cake. Refrigerate 45 minutes. Melt chocolate chips with 1 stick margarine and spread over cooled mint layer. Chill, then cut into small squares.

Date Oatmeal Bars

1/2 cup shortening
2/3 cup brown sugar, firmly packed
1 cup sifted flour
1 teaspoon salt
3/4 cup quick-cooking rolled oats
8 ounces pitted dates, cut
1/2 teaspoon cinnamon
6 1/2 ounces fluffy white frosting mix

Blend shortening, sugar, flour, salt and oats in medium-sized bowl until mixture is crumbly; press evenly into a 7 1/4 x 11 3/4 x 2-inch baking dish; top with layer of dates. Add cinnamon to frosting mix; prepare mix according to package directions. Spread frosting carefully over dates, sealing to edges of dish. Bake at 400° for 25 minutes, or until topping is golden brown. Cool; cut into bars.

Makes 12 bars

Dream Bars

1 cup flour
1/2 cup sugar
1/2 cup butter

Mix flour, sugar and butter; press in 8x8" pan and bake at 350° for 10 minutes while preparing the filling.

Filling

3 eggs
1 cup brown sugar
1 cup coconut
1/2 cup pecans
1 teaspoon vanilla

Beat eggs, add sugar gradually, then remaining ingredients. Pour over flour, sugar and butter mixture. Bake for 15 minutes more or until done.

Lace Cookies

1/2 pound butter
2 1/4 cups light brown sugar
2 1/4 cups quick-cook oats
3 tablespoons flour
1/2 teaspoon salt
1 teaspoon vanilla
1 egg, well beaten

Pour melted butter while piping hot over well-mixed ingredients, except egg and vanilla. Mix well; add egg and vanilla. Drop by teaspoonful on non-stick cookie sheet about 3 inches apart and bake at 375° for 10 minutes. Let cool one minute.

Makes 6 to 7 dozen cookies

Mrs. East's French Cookies

6 tablespoons butter
6 tablespoons sugar
1 teaspoon vanilla
2 eggs, separated
18 tablespoons flour
Pinch of baking powder
Strawberry jam
2 tablespoons sugar
Cinnamon
1/4 cup of finely chopped pecans,
   optional
Powdered sugar

Cream butter, sugar and vanilla. Add egg yolks,
flour and baking powder. Roll out thinly and cut
in circles or small squares. Put small dab of
strawberry jam on top of each cut out.
Beat egg whites until stiff; add sugar and cinnamon. Add pecans if desired. Place a teaspoon of
egg white mixture on top of strawberry jam topping and bake in a 300° oven until done. Do not
overcook. Sprinkle with powdered sugar.

These cookies are especially good.

Pecan Crispies

1 cup butter or margarine
1/2 cup sugar
1 teaspoon vanilla
1/2 cup crushed potato chips
1/2 cup chopped pecans
2 cups sifted flour

Cream butter, sugar and vanilla. Add crushed potato chips and pecans. Stir in flour. Roll into small balls. Place on ungreased cookie sheet and press ball flat with bottom of tumbler dipped in sugar. Bake at 350 degrees for 16 to 18 minutes or until lightly browned.

Makes 3 dozen cookies

Praline Cookies

24 graham cracker squares
1 1/2 cup pecans, chopped finely
1 cup light brown sugar, packed
1 cup butter

Place graham crackers close together on 12 x 15 cookie sheet or jelly roll pan; sprinkle pecans over crackers. Boil sugar and butter 4 minutes. Pour hot syrup over nuts. Bake at 325° for 8 to 10 minutes.

Aunt Maudie's Frozen Lemon Dessert

6 eggs, separated
1 1/2 cups granulated sugar
Juice of 6 lemons
1 tablespoon lemon rind, grated
Pinch salt
12-ounce can of
   Carnation evaporated milk, chilled
1 box vanilla wafers, crumbled

Combine beaten egg yolks, sugar, lemon juice, lemon rind and salt. Cook in top of double boiler, stirring constantly, until thickened. Remove from heat and chill. Beat egg whites until stiff. Beat Carnation milk until thick. Fold egg whites and carnation milk into chilled custard. Alternate layers of mixture with vanilla wafer crumbs in serving dish. Freeze and slice. Serve frozen.

Serves 12

When I was young, my Aunt Maude kept this in her deep freeze to serve when needed — which was very often! She still makes it for us to have in our deep freeze at our lake house.

Claudine's Coconut Mousse with Zabaglione Sauce

1 egg white
1 cup whipping cream
1/2 cup sugar
Dash of salt
1/8 teaspoon almond extract
1/4 teaspoon vanilla
1 cup flaked coconut, toasted

Place egg white and cream in small bowl and beat until stiff. Gradually add sugar and continue beating until blended. Fold in salt, flavorings and coconut. Spoon into freezing tray. Freeze about 2 to 3 hours. Serve with Zabaglione Sauce.

Zabaglione Sauce

1 1/4 cups cold milk
1/2 pint light cream
1 package vanilla instant pudding mix
1 egg white
2 tablespoons sugar
1/2 cup wine

Pour milk and cream in bowl. Add pudding mix and beat until well blended. Let stand 5 minutes to set. Beat egg white until stiff. Beat in sugar until smooth and glossy. Fold into pudding mix. Chill. Just before serving stir in wine.

Lemon Ice

3/4 cup lemon juice
2/3 cup granulated sugar
Grated rind of two lemons
Pinch of salt
1 1/2 cups milk
1/2 cup cream

Mix lemon juice, sugar, grated rind and salt.
Gradually stir into milk and cream. Freeze in ice
cube tray until firm. Remove from tray and beat
with electric mixer. Return to tray and freeze
until ready to serve.

Optional – Serve topped with raspberry sauce.

A nice tart dessert to serve after a heavy meal. Very attractive
served in stemmed sherbet or wine glasses.

Faith Langstaff's Brulee Ice Cream

4 egg yolks, beaten
Sugar
3/4 cup warm milk
3/4 cup sugar
1 quart milk

Beat as much sugar into egg yolks as they will take. Add egg yolk mixture to warm milk. Melt 3/4 cup sugar in iron skillet, stirring constantly, until melted and brown. Add melted sugar to milk mixture which must be hot to keep sugar from threading when it is added. Stir in milk but do not beat. Refrigerate overnight and freeze in hand freezer.

Makes about 1/2 gallon

Quick Raspberry Sherbet

6 ounces raspberry gelatin
2 cups boiling water
10-ounce package frozen raspberries
2 cups cold water
2 tablespoons lemon juice
2 egg whites
1/4 cup sugar

Dissolve gelatin in boiling water. Add frozen berries; stir until berries separate. Add cold water and lemon juice. Pour into 9x5x3-inch loaf pan. Freeze until firm, about 3 hours. Beat egg whites until foamy. Slowly add sugar, beating until stiff. Turn frozen gelatin into large mixing bowl, beat until mushy. Fold in meringue and spoon into loaf pan. Cover and return to freezer until firm, about 2 hours.

Serves 10 to 12

Zona's "Memaw's" Sherbet

1 carton half and half
1 medium can crushed pineapple
Strawberries as desired, fresh or frozen
1 cup orange juice
1/2 cup lemon juice
3 cups sugar
3 bananas, mashed
Whole milk

Mix all together, stirring to dissolve sugar. Pour into a 4-quart ice cream freezer and finish filling with whole milk. Freeze until firm.

Dennie's Summer Delight

3/4 cup graham cracker crumbs
1/4 cup melted butter
1 can sweetened condensed milk
2 egg yolks
2 tablespoons powdered chocolate
    drink mix
2 egg whites
4 tablespoons sugar, divided
1/2 pint whipping cream
1 tablespoon vanilla

Combine graham cracker crumbs and melted butter
for crust. Spread in a 9 x 9-inch pan and bake at
400° for 10 minutes. Cool. In a medium
saucepan, mix milk, egg yolks, and chocolate drink
mix. Cook over medium heat, stirring constantly
until sauce reaches a slow boil. Pour over crust
and cool completely. Whip egg whites with 2
tablespoons sugar until stiff peaks form. Set
aside. In a separate bowl, whip cream with remaining sugar and vanilla until firm. Fold together
cream and egg whites and spread over sauce.
Freeze overnight and serve frozen, cut in squares.

Serves 8

Almond Bisque

2 packages lemon gelatin
4 tablespoons sugar
1/2 teaspoon salt
2 cups boiling water
1 cup cold water
1 pint cream, whipped
1 teaspoon almond extract
12 macaroons, dried and rolled
18 marshmallows, cut in pieces
6 tablespoons chopped candied cherries
Angelica, optional

Dissolve gelatin, sugar and salt in boiling water.
Add cold water. Place bowl into larger container
of ice water to thicken gelatin mixture. Add
whipped cream and almond extract. Fold in
remaining ingredients. Pile the bisque into sherbet
or parfait glasses and garnish with cherries and
bits of angelica. Should be served very cold.

Serves 16

Apple Pinoche

4 to 5 cooking apples,
    peeled, cored and sliced
Lemon juice
1/2 cup sugar
Butter
3/4 cup whipping cream

Topping
8 ounces cream cheese
1/4 cup whipping cream

Dip sliced apples in lemon juice. Arrange apples in overlapping circles in a well-buttered ovenproof dish or quiche pan. Sprinkle with sugar and dot with butter. Bake at 350° for 45 minutes. Increase temperature to 400° and bake 15 minutes. Serve with topping.

For topping: Blend all ingredients and serve over apples.

*Low fat variation: Dot cholesterol-free butter over apples. Substitute reduced-fat cream cheese and fat-free milk for topping ingredients.

Strawberries & Cream Supreme

8 ounces cream cheese, softened
1 1/2 cups sour cream
6 tablespoons sugar
2 pints fresh strawberries, washed
  and hulled
1/4 cup light brown sugar

In small bowl, beat cream cheese until fluffy.
Add sour cream and sugar. Blend thoroughly.
Slice strawberries. Spoon cream cheese mixture
over berries. Spoon into stemmed glasses. Sprinkle
brown sugar over top. Refrigerate.

Serves 6 to 8

On a Saturday night following Christmas we did a wedding
reception for a very special bride. I went overboard on the size
of the cake. Very, very tall. I assembled it on the table early
and it was a masterpiece. Someone came in and said "I went
out to look at the cake and it wasn't on the table." I thought,
oh they looked at the wrong table. But, no! It had fallen to
the floor. Norma, being hostess on a very busy Saturday night,
came to the rescue. It was forty-five minutes before time for
guests to come into the room. A miracle was performed by
my "miracle worker." The cake was even lovelier the second
time around!

Pineapple Cream Loaf

1/2 cup butter
1 1/2 cups sifted powdered sugar
2 egg yolks
1/2 teaspoon lemon extract
18 3/4-ounce can crushed pineapple,
   drained
1 cup dairy sour cream
2 egg whites, stiffly beaten
8 lady fingers, split

Cream butter and sugar until fluffy. Add egg yolks, one at a time, beating well after each one. Stir in lemon extract and drained pineapple. Fold in sour cream and egg whites. Line bottom of 9x5x3-inch loaf pan with half of the lady fingers. Top with half of the pineapple mixture. Repeat layers. Place in refrigerator and chill overnight. Slice and serve.

Serves 8 to 10

This is an easy dessert to prepare in advance. Just remove from refrigerator, slice and serve.

Festive Pumpkin

1 medium size fresh pumpkin
8 peeled and chopped apples,
   dipped in lemon juice
Raisins
Dates, optional
Your favorite nuts
Cinnamon and/or nutmeg
2 cups sugar
6 pats of margarine

Select a pumpkin which does not have a hole in the
bottom. Cut a lid for top and clean insides, taking
out seeds. Mix apples with fruits, nuts, spices and
sugar. Fill pumpkin with this mixture and place
pats of margarine on top. Place lid on pumpkin and
cover stem with foil to prevent burning. Place
pumpkin on a foil-lined pan with low sides. Bake
at 250 degrees for 7 hours. After baking, pumpkin will remain warm for several hours. When
ready to serve, remove lid, scoop out the cooked
apple mixture along with cooked pumpkin from
inside and serve in a small dish or custard cup with
a dollop of whipped topping.

Serves 15 to 20

This recipe was a hit in Nashville when we served it at the
Southern Festival of Books where we rubbed elbows with Julia
Child.

Aunt Blanche's Strawberry Pizza

Crust
1 stick butter
1 cup flour
1/4 cup powdered sugar

Topping
1 pint fresh or frozen strawberries
4 tablespoons cornstarch
Red food coloring
8 ounces cream cheese
    at room temperature
1 can Eagle Brand milk
1/4 cup lemon juice

Melt butter, add sugar and flour, mix well. Pat crust in pizza pan or 8-inch pie pan. Bake at 325 degrees until brown. Cool.

Place strawberries and cornstarch in heavy saucepan and cook until thick, stirring constantly. Add red food coloring until desired shade of red. Set aside and cool. Combine cream cheese, Eagle Brand milk and lemon juice; beat well. Spread over crust. Top with cooled berries and chill.

Serves 6 to 8

Beehive Peach
with Bourbon Sauce

8 medium size peaches
Pie dough

Sauce
1 stick butter
2 cups sifted powdered sugar
1 teaspoon nutmeg
1 egg, beaten
1 or 2 jiggers of bourbon

Do not peel peaches or remove seeds. Place peaches, bud end down on cookie sheet and cover with strips of pie dough, starting on top, lapping strips 1/2 over the other, round and round, continuing until peach is covered. Brush with butter and sprinkle with granulated sugar. Bake for 5 to 10 minutes at 450°. Reduce heat to 325° and bake until nice and brown.

In heavy sauce pan, melt butter. Add powdered sugar, nutmeg and beaten egg. Be sure to add egg before the bourbon. Bring to simmer and add bourbon. Do not let boil. Spoon sauce over peach and serve.

If sauce is too thick, add a little water or bourbon.

Serves 8

Chocolate Almond Steamed Pudding

7 tablespoons unsalted butter
5 eggs, separated
1/2 cup sugar
9 tablespoons cocoa
1 1/2 cups ground almonds
2 tablespoons brandy

Spray a 1 1/2-quart pudding mold with nonstick spray; coat with sugar. Beat the butter until it is fluffy; beat in egg yolks, one at a time. Beat in the sugar, cocoa, almonds and brandy. Beat the egg whites until stiff and fold into the mixture. Spoon into prepared mold. Cover with greased foil and tie on securely. Stand the mold in a saucepan of hot water so the water comes two-thirds of the way up the sides of mold. Cover the pan and simmer one hour. Unmold immediately on to serving dish. When cool ice with Hard Sauce.

Hard Sauce

**5 tablespoons butter
1 cup confectioner's sugar
2 tablespoons Amaretto**

Cream the butter, then slowly add the sugar, beating with an electric beater until creamy and pale yellow. Add the Amaretto and blend.

Fire Logs

Old newspapers
3 gallons water
3 pounds rock salt
1 pound blue stone
Old containers

Roll papers into logs the size you like. Tie tightly with sturdy string. Heat water, rock salt and stone in old container. Mix together until melted. Place paper logs standing up in another old container and slowly pour liquid mixture over logs. Let stand until dry.

Caution:

Protect hands and arms while preparing and using liquid mixture and be careful of fumes from mixture. This should be prepared outside or with plenty of ventilation.

Blueberry Torte

16 graham crackers
1/2 cup sugar
1/4 cup butter, melted
8-ounce package cream cheese
1/2 cup sugar
1/2 teaspoon vanilla
2 eggs
1 can blueberries, drained,
   reserving juice
1/2 cup sugar
2 tablespoons cornstarch
1/4 cup water

Crush graham crackers and mix with melted butter and sugar. Press into 9x12-inch pyrex dish. Beat cream cheese, sugar, vanilla and eggs until creamy. Pour over cracker mixture and bake at 350° for 15 to 18 minutes.

Cook blueberry juice, water, sugar and cornstarch until thickened. Add drained blueberries and spread over cheese and cracker crumbs while still warm. Better if made the day before serving. Serve with whipped cream.

Serves 12 to 15

Chocolate Bread Pudding

1 quart milk
2 ounces unsweetened chocolate
2 cups bread crumbs
1/2 cup sugar
4 tablespoons butter, melted
2 eggs, slightly beaten
1/4 teaspoon salt
1 teaspoon vanilla

Preheat oven to 325°. Scald milk; break chocolate into pieces and stir into milk until melted and smooth. Soak bread crumbs in chocolate milk. Set aside to cool. Add sugar, butter, eggs, salt and vanilla. Mix well and pour into a buttered 2-quart baking dish. Bake 25 to 30 minutes. Serve warm or cool with whipped cream.

Serves 8 to 10

Glady's Caramel Dumplings

Sauce
2 tablespoons butter
1 1/2 cups brown sugar
1 1/2 cups boiling water
Dash salt

Place all ingredients in double boiler and boil gently for 5 minutes.

Dough
1 1/4 cup flour
1 1/2 teaspoon baking powder
1 1/3 cups sugar
1/2 teaspoon salt
2 tablespoons butter
1/3 cup milk
1/2 teaspoon vanilla

Sift dry ingredients: cut in butter. Add milk and vanilla. Mix and drop by teaspoons into boiling caramel sauce. Cover tightly and boil gently for 20 minutes without removing cover.

Lemon Curd

Grated peel and juice of four lemons
2 cups granulated sugar
2 cups butter
6 eggs, beaten
1/2 teaspoon salt

Place all ingredients in top of double boiler. Cook over boiling water, stirring constantly, for about 30 minutes or until consistency of thick cream sauce. Remove from heat and pour into serving dishes. Refrigerate for several hours before serving.

Optional - Top with whipped cream and garnish with thinly sliced lemon or lime.

Easy Boiled Custard

1 small package French vanilla
   instant pudding mix
4 cups milk
1/2 cup sugar
1 teaspoon vanilla
One 8-ounce carton whipped topping

Add pudding mix, sugar and vanilla to milk. Stir
until smooth. Fold in whipped topping. Chill until
very, very cold.

This dessert tastes like you may have spent a long time stirring it over a hot stove. We add apricot brandy to it for flavoring.

Miscellaneous

Curtis in Garden

Apricot Pineapple Marmalade

1 cup dried apricots, soaked
1 cup water
2 cups diced or grated pineapple
1/2 cup lemon juice
2 cups sugar

Mix apricots and water and cook slowly for 5 minutes. Add pineapple and cook for another 5 minutes. Add the remainder of the ingredients and cook until the marmalade thickens. Pour into sterilized jars and cover with paraffin.

Shirley Jean's Special Bird Food

1 cup peanut butter
1 cup shortening
1 cup all-purpose flour
4 cups plain cornmeal

Cream peanut butter and shortening. Add flour and cornmeal.

Birds will almost eat from your hand.

Zucchini Marmalade

6 cups peeled and shredded zucchini
1/2 cup lemon juice
1 cup crushed pineapple, drained
1 package Sure Jell
6 cups sugar
6 ounces apricot gelatin,
   or your favorite flavor

Cook zucchini for one hour on low heat. Add lemon juice, pineapple and Sure Jell and stir well. Add sugar and cook 6 minutes, then stir in gelatin while hot.

Pour into 4 one pint jars which have been sterilized, then seal.

Makes 4 pints

Pickled Pineapple

20-ounce can chunk pineapple
3/4 cup vinegar
1 cup sugar
6 all-spice berries
3 cloves
1 stick cinnamon
Dash salt

Drain pineapple, reserving 3/4 cup syrup. Add remaining ingredients to syrup and cook 15 minutes. Add pineapple and boil 5 minutes. For color you may add cinnamon candy.

Dog Biscuits

3/4 cup hot water or stock
1/3 cup margarine
1/2 cup evaporated milk
1/2 teaspoon salt
1 egg
3 cups whole wheat flour

Pour hot water over margarine in large bowl. Add remaining ingredients. Shape mixture into dog biscuits.

I make these every year for our church's Blessing of the Animals.

Norma's Chunk Pickles

Cucumbers
1 cup salt
Boiling water
3 tablespoons powdered alum
5 pints vinegar
6 cups sugar

Slice cucumbers in chunk pieces and fill a gallon jar.
Add salt and fill with boiling water. Let set for 6
days. Pour off salt water and wash cucumbers.
Replace in gallon jar and fill with boiling water.
Let set for 24 hours. Pour off water and add
alum to cucumbers. Cover with boiling water. Let
set for 24 hours. Drain and place in jars. Mix
vinegar and sugar. Bring to a boil and pour over
cucumbers and seal.

Encore

Mail to:
McClanahan Publishing House, Inc.
P. O. Box 100
Kuttawa, KY 42055

For Orders call TOLL FREE
1-800-544-6959
Visa & MasterCard accepted

Please send me _____ copies of

Encore @ $ 21.95 each   _____
Postage & handling   4.00   _____
Kentucky residents add 6% sales tax@ 1.32 each   _____

Total enclosed   _____

Make check payable to McClanahan Publishing House

Ship to:
NAME
_____

ADDRESS
_____

CITY _____ STATE _____

ZIP _____